T0372311

Cambridge Elements

Elements in Epistemology
edited by
Stephen Hetherington
University of New South Wales, Sydney

DISAGREEMENT

Diego E. Machuca
National Council for Scientific and Technical
Research

CAMBRIDGE
UNIVERSITY PRESS

Shaftesbury Road, Cambridge CB2 8EA, United Kingdom

One Liberty Plaza, 20th Floor, New York, NY 10006, USA

477 Williamstown Road, Port Melbourne, VIC 3207, Australia

314–321, 3rd Floor, Plot 3, Splendor Forum, Jasola District Centre,
New Delhi – 110025, India

103 Penang Road, #05–06/07, Visioncrest Commercial, Singapore 238467

Cambridge University Press is part of Cambridge University Press & Assessment,
a department of the University of Cambridge.

We share the University's mission to contribute to society through the pursuit of
education, learning and research at the highest international levels of excellence.

www.cambridge.org
Information on this title: www.cambridge.org/9781009539289

DOI: 10.1017/9781009324458

When citing this work, please include a reference to the DOI 10.1017/9781009324458

First published 2024

A catalogue record for this publication is available from the British Library

ISBN 978-1-009-53928-9 Hardback
ISBN 978-1-009-32443-4 Paperback
ISSN 2398-0567 (online)
ISSN 2514-3832 (print)

Disagreement

Elements in Epistemology

DOI: 10.1017/9781009324458
First published online: December 2024

Diego E. Machuca
National Council for Scientific and Technical Research
Author for correspondence: Diego E. Machuca, diegomachuca@gmail.com

Abstract: This Element engages with the epistemic significance of disagreement, focusing on its skeptical implications. It examines various types of disagreement-motivated skepticism in ancient philosophy, ethics, philosophy of religion, and general epistemology. In each case, it favors suspension of judgment as the seemingly appropriate response to the realization of disagreement. One main line of argument pursued in the Element is that, since in real-life disputes we have limited or inaccurate information about both our own epistemic standing and the epistemic standing of our dissenters, personal information and self-trust can rarely function as symmetry breakers in favor of our own views.

Keywords: peer disagreement, skepticism, suspension of judgment, bias, first-person perspective

ISBNs: 9781009539289 (HB), 9781009324434 (PB), 9781009324458 (OC)
ISSNs: 2398-0567 (online), 2514-3832 (print)

Contents

Preface

My interest in the phenomenon of disagreement and its epistemic implications has always gone hand in hand with a fascination with skepticism, particularly of a Pyrrhonian stripe. For this reason, the stance on the epistemic significance of disagreement adopted in the present Element is skeptical. Even though many academics examine the philosophical import of skepticism, very few are skeptics – let alone radical skeptics. Part of the modest value of the Element might then lie in its approaching disagreement from an unpopular perspective.

1 Introduction

Disagreement reigns in our lives. There is no escape from it even if we avoid interacting with others. For, in addition to being confronted with individuals who do not share our views or being onlookers to other people's disputes on a daily basis, we often disagree with our own past or present self. The inevitability of inter- or intrapersonal disagreement and the importance we assign to many controversial matters should be reason enough to explore the epistemic and practical implications of disagreement. This Element focuses exclusively on its epistemic significance.

With respect to interpersonal disagreement, even though we may feel quite confident that we are right vis-à-vis any specific controversial matter and even though we may regard such confidence as well-founded, we should start having serious doubts about the correctness of our views and the reasonability of our confidence if we consider the fact that we are involved in countless interpersonal disagreements. Otherwise, we should conclude that we are most of the time right about controversial matters and that our dissenters get things wrong with astonishing frequency. This would be plausible if we were highly reliable thinkers on a wide range of topics and were usually surrounded by fools. It is hard to accept that either case obtains, though. But even if we could legitimately claim that we are mostly right and our dissenters mostly wrong, disagreement would give us the opportunity to learn something of philosophical interest about the latter's epistemic standing: their incorrect views may be due, for example, to their being under the unconscious influence of cognitive or motivational biases or other epistemically distorting factors.

As for those interpersonal disputes to which we are onlookers, disagreement presents us with the challenge of coming up with a reliable way to decide which of the disagreeing parties, if any, is right. This is particularly demanding when all parties strike us as being intelligent and knowledgeable to roughly the same degree or when we are not in position to determine how intelligent and knowledgeable they are. Are there certain epistemic criteria that enable us to reliably make that kind of decision? Are we trustworthy enough to discern which epistemic criteria are correct? Are any proposed criteria bound to fall prey to the problem of the regress of justification?

The view of a systematic epistemic asymmetry in our favor becomes irrelevant when we set aside our disagreement with others and focus on our own beliefs and the conflicts we detect among them; that is, when we focus on both synchronic and diachronic intrapersonal disagreements. For, first, we sometimes discover that, at the present time, we hold inconsistent beliefs about a given matter. Second, we sometimes disagree with our own past self, and although we typically claim that our present belief is the result of an improvement in our epistemic position, such an alleged improvement shows us that we are susceptible to being wrong about controversial issues – or at least that we were so susceptible, which raises the question of why that may not happen to us again. Third, from time to time we notice variability in our opinions and resulting decisions that cannot in good faith be explained by the consideration of epistemically relevant factors: we give money to a homeless person or refrain from doing so depending on our mood, we give low or high grades to exams and assignments depending on the time of the day, or we give mild or harsh sentences to a defendant depending on whether our basketball team lost last night. The question then arises: if we are susceptible to falling prey to such epistemically irrelevant and distorting factors when it comes to our own divergent opinions and decisions, why would we not be equally susceptible to falling prey to those factors when it comes to opinions and decisions of ours that are rejected by others?

In line with the social turn in general epistemology, over the past twenty years there has been an explosion of interest in the epistemic significance of disagreement – particularly disagreement between so-called epistemic peers. Upon discovering that someone disagrees with you, should you conciliate and considerably lower your degree of confidence in your belief or even adopt the other person's belief, or should you rather remain steadfast and retain your belief with the same, or a slightly decreased, degree of confidence? The present Element offers a brief critical overview of the debate on the significance of disagreement in analytic epistemology and argues that the prospects for resolving disagreements in a rational manner appear rather dim.[1] But before doing so, the Element looks at the treatment of disagreement both in ancient philosophy and in

---

[1] By "resolving a disagreement in a rational manner," I mean that, by sharing and weighing the reasons for the conflicting views on p, (i) the disputants rationally reach a consensus on where the truth about whether p (probably) lies, or (ii) from a first-person perspective, one rationally decides where the truth about whether p (probably) lies, even if one's opponent is unable to see it, or (iii) an onlooker rationally decides where the truth about whether p (probably) lies, even if the disputants themselves fail to recognize it. In the case of (ii) or (iii), there is no resolution of the disagreement in the sense that the disputants have not reached a shared view, but there is

contemporary ethics and philosophy of religion. The reason is that therein we find stances that are philosophically worth exploring and that are relevant to the connection between disagreement and skepticism, which is the focus of this Element. In addition, the immediate antecedent of the extensive discussion of disagreement in general epistemology is to be found in the discussion of disagreement in religious epistemology.

Here is a bird's-eye view of the Element. Section 2 is devoted to the discussion of disagreement in ancient skepticism. I first present, in Section 2.1, the disagreement-based skepticism of the ancient Pyrrhonists. An important part of the Pyrrhonian strategy consisted in appealing to the so-called Agrippan trilemma to show that the disagreeing parties are epistemically on a par. One reason why considering the Pyrrhonists' strategy is useful for the current debate on the epistemic significance of disagreement is that, although the Pyrrhonists typically used Agrippa's trilemma in combination with the mode from disagreement, most present-day epistemological discussions of disagreement make no reference to the trilemma; and, conversely, in most current analyses of the Agrippan trilemma, disagreement is set aside. In Section 2.2, I examine the views on disagreement of Academic skeptics and medical Empiricists. The importance of their discussion of disagreement lies in the fact that both groups drew a second-order epistemological conclusion from the existence of unresolvable disputes, a conclusion we do not find among those drawn in current epistemological analyses of disagreement.

Sections 3 and 4 deal, respectively, with moral and religious disagreement, focusing on both arguments for a negative ontological conclusion and arguments for an agnostic epistemological conclusion. In epistemological parlance, the first type of argument intends to provide a rebutting defeater, while the second intends to provide an undercutting defeater.[2] With regard to religious disagreement, two other topics that are addressed are the debate between exclusivists, pluralists, and inclusivists, and the epistemic significance of religious experience.

Section 5 focuses on the discussion of disagreement in contemporary analytic epistemology. Section 5.1 presents the notion of epistemic peerhood. Section 5.2 offers an overview of the current debate between conciliationists and steadfasters. Section 5.3 presents two related strategies that have been proposed for resolving disagreements: the appeal to the inevitability of the first-person perspective and the self-trust that comes with it; and the appeal to the information one possesses about one's own epistemic situation and the high degree of justified confidence in one's own belief. A problem faced by such

---

resolution in the sense that a rational decision about whether p has been made (cf. Barnes 1990: 30–31).

[2] Succinctly put, while a rebutting defeater for p is a reason to disbelieve p, an undercutting defeater for p is a reason that undermines the connection between p and one's evidence for p.

strategies is that, from a first-person perspective, there seems to be a dialectical-cum-epistemic symmetry between the disputants. Sections 5.4 and 5.5 argue that another problem faced by those two strategies concerns the limited or misleading information we possess both about ourselves and about our dissenters, which prevents us from determining who is in a better epistemic position with regard to the disputed issue. Section 5.4 reviews part of the abundant evidence provided by cognitive psychology to the effect that our self-knowledge is limited and to a large extent inaccurate: we often overestimate our cognitive capacities, we tend to confabulate about the reasons for our judgments and decisions, we mistakenly believe that others are more susceptible to bias than we are, we often fall prey to confirmation bias, and there is a non-negligible amount of occasion noise in our judgments. Section 5.5 argues that, in real-life disputes, one usually lacks information about the quality of one's opponent's evidence, the general reliability of his cognitive capacities, and the functioning of those capacities in the specific circumstance of the disagreement. Finally, Section 5.6 briefly discusses a *sui generis* view, "skeptical dogmatism," that has recently been defended in the epistemology of disagreement literature.

Section 6 draws the Element to a close by summarizing the various ways in which acknowledged disagreement may be epistemically significant.

2 Ancient Skepticism

The discussion of the ancient skeptics' treatment of disagreement is divided into two parts, the first dealing with the Pyrrhonism of Sextus Empiricus and the second with so-called Academic skepticism and with medical Empiricism.

2.1 Pyrrhonism

Sextus was a skeptical doctor whose *floruit* seems to have been in the early third century CE. His substantial extant writings are our main source for ancient Pyrrhonism. This brand of skepticism is defined by the following attitudes, practices, and problems: wide-ranging suspension of judgment, engagement in open-minded inquiry into truth, emphasis on the existence of widespread and entrenched disagreements, the problem of the criterion of truth and that of the regress of justification, and taking what appears (or the way one is appeared to) as the guide to practical decisions and philosophical investigation.[3]

In the first book of his *Pyrrhonian Outlines* (henceforth *PH*, the initials of the Greek title in transliteration), Sextus expounds three sets of "modes" of

---

[3] I do not include in this list the pursuit and the attainment of undisturbedness for reasons laid out in Machuca (2006, 2020).

argumentation by means of which suspension of judgment is supposed to be induced: the Ten Modes (*PH* I 35–163), the Five Modes (*PH* I 164–177), and the Two Modes (*PH* I 178–179). The Five Modes are attributed to Agrippa by Diogenes Laertius (DL IX 88) and are the most lethal weapons of the skeptical arsenal due to their apparent intuitiveness and universal scope. They are disagreement, infinite regress, relativity, hypothesis, and reciprocity. Sextus expounds them as follows:

> The mode deriving from disagreement is that by means of which we discover that, with regard to the matter proposed, there has arisen, both in ordinary life and among philosophers, an undecidable dispute owing to which we end up with suspension of judgment, since we are not able to choose or to reject anything. The mode deriving from regress *ad infinitum* is that in which we say that what is offered as a warrant for the matter proposed needs another warrant, and this latter needs another, and so on *ad infinitum*, so that, given that we have nowhere from which to begin to establish it, suspension of judgment follows. The mode deriving from relativity, as we said before, is that in which the underlying object appears thus and so relative to what does the judging and to the things observed together with it, but we suspend judgment about what it is like in relation to nature. The mode deriving from hypothesis is that which arises whenever the dogmatists, being thrown back *ad infinitum*, begin from something that they do not establish, but that they deem worthy to assume simply and without proof by virtue of a concession. The reciprocal mode arises whenever that which ought to be confirmatory of the matter investigated needs a warrant from what is investigated. In this case, as we are not able to take either to establish the other, we suspend judgment about both. (*PH* I 165–169; my translation.)

The modes of hypothesis, reciprocity, and infinite regress constitute what in contemporary philosophy is known as "Agrippa's trilemma." Much of recent epistemology is devoted to responding to the trilemma – mainly under the label "the epistemic regress problem" or "the problem of the regress of justification." Each of those three modes targets a specific justificatory strategy: the mode of hypothesis targets the view that some beliefs are basic or self-justifying; the mode of reciprocity targets the view that a belief is justified provided it is part of a system of mutually supporting beliefs; and the mode of infinite regress targets the view that a belief is justified provided it is supported by an infinite chain of non-repeating reasons. Although Sextus says or implies that each of the three modes can induce suspension separately, the immediately following passage (*PH* I 170–177) – in which he explains the way the Agrippan modes bring about suspension regarding every object of investigation – makes it clear that suspension can be induced more effectively when they work in tandem (see Barnes 1990). This is reasonable because, although one can imagine that someone adopting one of the above strategies may suspend judgment after being confronted with the corresponding mode, he will more probably appeal to the other strategies to find an alternative way to justify his beliefs.

With respect to the mode from disagreement, the mere existence of a disagreement does not of course justify suspending judgment, because one may come to the conclusion that one of the conflicting views is to be preferred to the others due to its superior epistemic credentials. This is why, when presenting that mode, Sextus speaks of "undecidable" or "unresolvable" dispute: it is the fact that one has so far been unable to resolve the dispute about whether p that leads one to suspend judgment about whether p.[4] Now, it may be argued that one's inability to resolve the dispute about whether p is the result of the use of the Agrippan trilemma to show that any attempt to rationally justify one of conflicting views on p fails. If that were the case, the disagreement mode should be regarded as a two-step strategy: (i) presentation of a dispute and (ii) application of the trilemma to show that the dispute cannot be settled. When applied to a disagreement, the modes of hypothesis, reciprocity, and infinite regress work in tandem: when someone attempts to escape from one of those modes in his effort to justify his view on the disputed matter, he falls into one of the other two. The trilemma shows that the conflicting views fare equally badly as far as their justificatory standing is concerned. Since all the disagreeing parties get caught in the trap set by those modes, one must suspend judgment about which of the conflicting views, if any, is correct.

Note that, even if there is no disagreement about whether p, one may ask how the shared belief that p (or that not-p) is justified and then attack, by means of the trilemma, the different strategies purporting to provide the desired justification. If one realizes that one is unable to justify the belief that p, then one is (rationally or psychologically) constrained to suspend judgment about whether p. The interpretation of the mode from disagreement as a complex argumentative strategy discussed in the previous paragraph already presented the Agrippan trilemma as the core of that strategy, with disagreement only providing the material upon which the trilemma works. The point made in this paragraph is stronger inasmuch as it calls attention to the fact that suspension can be induced in the absence of a dispute. This may lead one to view disagreement

---

[4] It should be emphasized that the Pyrrhonist does not claim that a disagreement is unresolvable because the disputants would not resolve it even if, e.g., they were to turn to all available evidence or even if they were to use all available means to enhance their reasoning abilities and discover and eliminate whatever biases might infect their ability to assess evidence. Rather, he limits himself to reporting that the parties to the disagreement about whether p have so far been unable to reach a consensus on which attitude towards the question whether p is epistemically rational, and that he himself has so far been unable to decide which attitude is epistemically rational by weighing the reasons for and against p.

"as a psychologically useful aid to the sceptic" rather than as "an epistemologically necessary condition for the generation of scepticism" (Barnes 1990: 116). In the absence of disagreement, one might erroneously think that "there was no room or reason for doubt, that [one was] justified in assenting to the opinion insofar as there was no dissentient voice. Hence the observation of disagreement is pertinent to Pyrrhonism: it draws attention to the fact that assent should not be given without ado – doubt *might* be raised because doubts *have* been raised" (Barnes 1990: 116, italics in the original).

Even though I agree that Agrippa's trilemma can induce suspension independently of the existence of a dispute, I do not think that disagreement is merely a psychological aid. There are at least three reasons to view disagreement as one of the keys to the generation of skepticism. First, for some epistemologists, one is under no obligation to give reasons for one's belief that p in the absence of a concrete challenge to its epistemic credentials. The existence of a disagreement about whether p can be taken to constitute such a challenge. For example, if two persons who take themselves to be roughly evidential and cognitive equals with respect to whether p discover that they disagree about whether p, they can take this disagreement as higher-order evidence that they may have made a mistake when assessing the first-order evidence bearing on whether p (more on this in Section 5). The disagreement can then be taken as a challenge for the disputants to provide reasons for their conflicting beliefs about whether p. In such a scenario, one can have recourse to the Agrippan trilemma to show that, in the end, neither disputant can justify his belief about whether p and, hence, that their beliefs are epistemically on a par.

Second, the mode from disagreement can lead to suspension without the application of the trilemma. Faced with the disagreement about whether p, a person may assess the arguments for and against p and find them equally strong, thereby suspending judgment about whether p, without realizing that both the attempt to justify belief in p and the attempt to justify belief in not-p lead to the epistemic regress problem. In several passages in which he does not appeal to the trilemma, Sextus says that the Pyrrhonist is compelled to suspend judgment in the face of an unresolvable disagreement. For example, in concluding his exposition of the Tenth Mode, which deals mainly with moral disagreements, Sextus remarks that, given that we are unable to say what each object is like in its nature but only how it appears in relation to various factors, we must suspend judgment about what things are really like (*PH* I 145–163). The mode from disagreement should not therefore be deemed to be a complex argumentative strategy that necessarily relies on the Agrippan trilemma – contrary to the interpretation sketched above.

Third, when dealing with certain general epistemological theories that offer solutions to Agrippa's trilemma, the Pyrrhonist cannot make use of the trilemma to reply to those theories without begging the question, but he can still appeal to the mode from disagreement. Let me explain. Some epistemologists have objected that the trilemma rests on controversial presuppositions: in their view, it is based on a conception of justification that is not universally shared or it distorts our everyday epistemic practices (see, e.g., Williams 2004 and Klein 2011). Faced with such objections, the Pyrrhonist would remark that there are long-standing and entrenched disagreements between the proponents of the various epistemological theories – including the dispute about what exactly is questionable about the Agrippan trilemma – and would press them to explain how those disagreements are to be resolved. How are we supposed to rationally settle the dispute between, for example, foundationalists, coherentists, and infinitists, given that there seem to be no discernible epistemic differences between the three groups taken as a whole? For the members of the different groups seem to be competent epistemologists who are familiar with the relevant arguments and theories concerning justification, and they are all aware of the pertinent conceptual analyses and distinctions. To make matters worse, within each group the members are far from agreeing, so that we also need to find a reliable touchstone for choosing between the different variants of the same general theories. Likewise, confronted with the claim that the epistemological ideas underlying the Agrippan trilemma distort some aspects of our ordinary epistemic procedures, the Pyrrhonist would argue that we are faced with two conflicting conceptions of justification (philosophical and ordinary), and that this conflict cannot be resolved by assuming arbitrarily that our everyday epistemic practices are to be preferred. Thus, awareness of disagreement is still epistemically significant and may lead us to suspend judgment, even without appeal to Agrippa's trilemma.

In sum, the mode from disagreement poses a serious challenge to the epistemic credentials of our beliefs independently of Agrippa's trilemma and should not be considered a mere psychological aid. This is the reason why ancient Pyrrhonists laid so much emphasis on the existence of widespread and persistent ordinary and philosophical disagreements. They also called attention to the fact that, when trying to find a way to resolve a given disagreement, we encounter further disagreements, sometimes high-order ones that concern even trickier questions. Disagreement is a phenomenon that keeps reemerging at different levels.[5]

---

[5] Here nothing has been said about the relativity mode, but see Machuca (2022: 86–87).

2.2 Academic Skepticism and Medical Empiricism

Plato's Academy had a skeptical phase, whose main representatives were Arcesilaus (316/5–241/0 BCE) and Carneades (214–129/8 BCE). Academic skeptics are said (i) to have denied that things are apprehensible (i.e., knowable) or that the truth can be found,[6] and (ii) to have suspended judgment about everything or withheld all assent.[7] These two stances are sometimes related in our sources: across-the-board suspension or total withholding of assent stems from the recognition that everything is inapprehensible (*Acad.* I 45, II 78; *Praep. evang.* XIV.4.15; *C. Acad.* II.5.11, 6.14). This may be interpreted in the sense that suspension about all first-order matters follows from the second-order view that the truth about such matters cannot be known: if it is not possible to know what things are like either because we are cognitively limited (*Acad.* I 44, *Praep. evang.* XIV.4.15) or because truth itself is hidden (*Acad.* I 44–45, *C. Acad.* II.5.12), then one cannot but suspend judgment about what any given thing is like.[8] Another idea underlying the view that one should suspend judgment in the face of inapprehensibility is that assent should be given only to what is known inasmuch as holding mere opinions is rash, vicious, and dangerous (*Acad.* I 45, II 68; *C. Acad.* II 6.14). It is also sometimes reported that, for the Academics, suspension about whether *p* results from the fact that the arguments for and against *p* are of equal strength (*Acad.* I 45, *Praep. evang.* XIV.4.15; cf. DL IV 28, *Acad.* II 124, 133).

In that connection, it should be noted that the Academics called attention to the skeptical implications of disagreement – specifically, of philosophical disputes – as is attested mainly in Cicero's *Academica* II 114–146. After observing that the champion of each philosophical system claims that one must endorse it because only the doctrines in that system are true, and that such a claim is a sign of arrogance (*Acad.* II 114–115), Cicero reviews disagreements in physics (*Acad.* II 116–128), ethics (*Acad.* II 129–141), and logic (*Acad.* II 142–146). Regarding physics, he remarks that one needs to decide which of the arguments put forward by the physicists to believe, since it is not possible to choose more than one, and he focuses on the "extreme disagreement

---

[6] See Cicero, *Academica* I 45, II 18, 66, 68, 73, 83, 102, 112, 148, *De oratore* III 67; Plutarch, *Adversus Colotem* 1122A; Sextus, *PH* I 3, 226; Eusebius, *Praeparatio evangelica* XIV.4.15; Augustine, *Contra Academicos* I.3.7, II.5.11–12, 9.23, 13.30, III.1.1, 3.5, 5.12, 9.18, 10.21–23, 16.36.

[7] See *Acad.* I 45, II 59; *Adv. Col.* 1122A; *PH* I 232; DL IV 28, 32; *Praep. evang.* XIV.4.15, 7.15; *C. Acad.* II.5.11–12, 13.30, III.5.11–12, 10.22, 16.35.

[8] The view that unknowability leads to suspension can be related to the knowledge norm of belief endorsed by some contemporary philosophers. According to that norm, one may believe that *p* only if one knows that *p*. Hence, if one is aware that the truth about *p* is unknowable, then one is aware that one does not know whether *p* and so one may not believe that *p* or that not-*p*, i.e., one must suspend belief about whether *p*.

among the leading men" about "the principles of things out of which everything is constituted" (*Acad.* II 117; my translation). Cicero's review of that disagreement makes it clear that he thinks that it is not possible to resolve it. Part of the reason may be that they are all "leading men," and so that they are epistemic equals or that the epistemic differences between them are negligible (cf. Cicero, *De natura deorum* [*ND*] I 14). Now, at one point, Cicero remarks that he assents to neither of the rival views on whether god created everything for our sakes because sometimes one of them seems more persuasive and sometimes the other does (*Acad.* II 121, cf. II 134). Although one might interpret this remark in the sense that the Academic skeptic successively believes the view that strikes him as more persuasive at each moment, Cicero's point seems to be that one cannot believe any of the conflicting views because, at the end of the day, none of them takes precedence over the others as far as their persuasiveness is concerned. In this connection, when referring to the disagreements about the nature of the mind and the body, Cicero points out: "Many things are said on either side. One of them seems certain to your sage, but to ours it does not occur which one is most persuasive, so equally weighty are, in most cases, the opposite reasons" (*Acad.* II 124). And when reviewing ethical disagreements, Cicero asks whether he should pick one of the conflicting views even when the arguments "on either side seem to [him] acute and equally weighty" (*Acad.* II 133). These passages indicate that, when confronted with disagreements between equally persuasive views, the Academic withholds assent – or is in doubt, as Augustine remarks at *Contra Academicos* III.7.16 (see also *ND* I 1, 14).

Other passages indicate that the Academic also draws a negative epistemological conclusion from the existence of disagreements between equally persuasive views, namely, that it is impossible to apprehend the truth about the disputed matters. For example, in the passage immediately following *Academica* II 121 (referred to above), Cicero observes: "All these things are hidden, Lucullus, concealed and surrounded by thick darkness, so that no human intellect is acute enough to penetrate the sky or enter into the earth" (*Acad.* II 122). And when reviewing the disagreement among the physicists about the first principles, Cicero says that perhaps the doctrines of one of them are true, for he allows that there is something true, but that he does not accept that they are apprehended (*Acad.* II 119). The reason why the possibly true doctrines are not apprehended is clearly that the truth cannot be known. The inapprehensibility of truth is then the reason why one cannot choose among the conflicting views: supposing that one of them is true, since one cannot know that it is true, one cannot accept it and reject the others. Note also that Augustine tells us that, in defense of the view that the truth cannot be found, the Academics appeal to, among other things, the disagreements among philosophers (*C. Acad.* II.5.11; see also III.10.23).

How are we to reconcile the claim that the recognition of disagreement between equally persuasive positions leads one to suspend judgment about whether p with the claim that it leads one to affirm that the truth about p is unknowable? The two claims are not incompatible, for the former is first-order while the latter is second-order. Note that the Academic skeptic may well suspend judgment in the face of a *specific* disagreement when the conflicting positions strike him as equally strong, and also suspend judgment on account of the second-order *general* view about the inapprehensibility of the truth about the disagreed upon issues. Both may well be sufficient reasons to suspend judgment. In this connection, at *Acad.* I 45 Cicero tells us that "by arguing against everyone's opinions, [Arcesilaus] led most people away from their own opinions, given that, when on the same matter equally weighty reasons were found for the opposite sides, assent was *more easily* withheld from either side" (emphasis added). This passage may be interpreted as saying that, even though suspension is required by the view of the inapprehensibility of truth, the equal weight of the conflicting views on whether p – which is, after all, nothing but a sign that reveals the inapprehensibility of the truth about p – makes it *psychologically easier* to suspend judgment.

The link between the observation of unresolvable disagreement and the affirmation of the inapprehensibility of truth is more explicit among adherents of medical Empiricism, which was one of the three main Hellenistic and Imperial medical sects and had a close connection with Pyrrhonism. In *On the Sects for Beginners*, Galen (129–216 CE) remarks that the Empiricists maintain that the disagreement among the dogmatists about non-evident things is unresolvable, and that inapprehensibility is the cause of unresolvable disagreement and that this kind of disagreement is, in turn, the sign of inapprehensibility (11–12, ed. Helmreich). Similarly, in the preface to his work *On Medicine*, Celsus (25 BCE–50 CE) points out that, according to the Empiricists, nature is inapprehensible and that it cannot be apprehended is plain from the disagreement among philosophers and doctors about non-evident causes and natural functions – a disagreement that cannot be resolved (*Praefatio* 27–28).

Why would the existence of unresolvable disagreements be a sign that the disagreed upon matters are inapprehensible? One possible answer consists in interpreting the thesis of inapprehensibility as the conclusion of an inference to the best explanation: given that the disagreement about whether p has existed for a long time and remains undecidable despite all the attempts at resolution by meticulous and intelligent thinkers, the most plausible explanation is that it is impossible for us to know what is really the case regarding the question whether p. This may be understood as referring either to a constitutive cognitive limitation of humans or to the fact that the matter under consideration is of such a nature that it cannot be known.

The view of Academics and medical Empiricists is no doubt skeptical inasmuch as it calls into question our beliefs about p. The Pyrrhonist's skeptical stance is more cautious inasmuch as he regards the inapprehensibility thesis as one possible explanation of the existence of the long-running unresolvable disagreement about whether p that is not more plausible than, for example, the view that one of the disputants is right while the others are blind to the evidence because of the influence of certain biases, or the view that none of the disputants is right but that the dispute will be settled at some point because the truth about p will be discovered. When contrasting the Pyrrhonian outlook with that of the Academics Carneades and Clitomachus, Sextus remarks that the Pyrrhonist "expects it to be possible for some things to be apprehended" (*PH* I 226). Thus, the difference between Pyrrhonists, on the one hand, and Academics and medical Empiricists, on the other, concerns the higher-order question of whether knowledge of the truth about disputed matters is possible. For, given that they all regard the disagreement about the first-order question whether p as unresolvable in the sense that one is (at this point) unable to take a stand on that question, they all agree that one is to suspend judgment about whether p. The Pyrrhonist limits himself to saying that one has *so far* been unable to take a stand on the question whether p; he makes no claims about what might happen in the future. It is his meta-agnosticism about the possibility of knowledge that enables him to engage in continuing open-minded inquiry into truth (*PH* I 1–3, II 11).

I hope that the brief presentation of ancient skeptical approaches to disagreement will give a rough idea of stances that are not common in present-day discussions of disagreement and that are worth exploring as alternative reactions to that phenomenon. One key difference is that the disagreement-based skepticism found in ancient philosophy is much more wide-ranging than the disagreement-based skepticism found in contemporary philosophy.

3 Moral Disagreement

The skeptical implications of disagreement have since long been much debated in contemporary metaethics. The main focus of attention has been on whether the existence of deep, widespread, and persistent moral disputes shows that robust moral realism is false.[9] Consider John Leslie Mackie's moral error

---

[9] Robust moral realism maintains that (i) moral judgments are truth-apt, (ii) some of them are true by virtue of the mind-independent moral facts or properties that those judgments track, and (iii) moral facts and properties are non-natural (inasmuch as they are intrinsically prescriptive) and causally inert.

theory, according to which first-order moral judgments are truth-apt because they are assertions that attribute moral properties to objects, but they are all false because such properties are not instantiated. Mackie based his theory on two arguments: the argument from queerness and the argument from relativity, which is in fact an argument from disagreement. His version of the latter argument includes a best-explanation premise: "the actual variations in the moral codes are more readily explained by the hypothesis that they reflect ways of life than by the hypothesis that they express perceptions, most of them seriously inadequate and badly distorted, of objective values" (Mackie 1977: 37). Mackie's moral disagreement argument could be formulated thus:

1. There exist deep, widespread, and persistent disagreements about moral matters.
2. Such disagreements are best explained as resulting from variations in ways of life rather than from variations in perceptions of alleged objective moral values, facts, or properties.
3. If objective moral values, facts, or properties are explanatorily redundant, then they do not exist.

Therefore:

4. There are no objective moral values, facts, or properties.

This argument can be regarded as a combination of an argument from disagreement and an argument from the best explanation, and so it could be called "the argument from the best explanation of disagreement." The role of disagreement is not irrelevant, since it is what raises the challenge for the moral realist: there is a phenomenon that needs to be accounted for. Notice that Mackie's ontological version of the moral disagreement argument is epistemically relevant inasmuch as, if there are no objective moral values, facts, or properties, then moral knowledge is undermined – at least moral knowledge understood in a robustly realist way.[10] The argument purports to provide a rebutting defeater for our first-order moral beliefs – as already noted, Mackie's moral error theory maintains that all first-order moral judgments are false. Notice, finally, that premise 3 is based on a principle of parsimony according to which one should not unnecessarily multiply entities: if a kind of entity is not necessary for explaining a given phenomenon, then one should deny its existence. That explanatory redundancy or dispensability suffices by itself to assert that something does not exist is

---

[10] To be precise, first-order moral knowledge is undermined – which makes the moral error theory a form of skepticism – whereas metaethical knowledge is still possible. For instance, the moral error theorist claims to know that there are no objective moral values, facts, or properties – and so, in this respect, his stance is not skeptical.

no doubt questionable, and so it seems that premise 3 should instead be couched in epistemological terms: if certain facts are explanatorily redundant or dispensable, then one has no reason to believe in their existence and should therefore suspend judgment. If premise 3 were thus couched, the argument would provide an undercutting defeater for our first-order moral beliefs rather than a rebutting defeater: those beliefs are unjustified (either *per se* or up to this point) rather than false. This epistemological version of the moral disagreement argument is much more plausible than the ontological version.

Another plausible version of the moral disagreement argument also provides an undercutting defeater by emphasizing the (as yet) impossibility of coming up with a rational way to resolve moral disputes, and concludes that conflicting moral beliefs are not epistemically justified or do not amount to knowledge either *per se* or up to this point. Here's a possible formulation of the argument, focusing on epistemic justification:

[1] There exist deep, widespread, and persistent first-order moral disagreements.
[2] There is (as yet) no rational way to resolve such disagreements.

Therefore:

[3] Conflicting first-order moral beliefs are not epistemically justified *per se* or up to this point.

The (as yet) impossibility of rationally resolving moral disagreements may be due to different reasons: the apparent epistemic parity between the disagreeing parties, the lack of an agreed-upon epistemic criterion, or the inability to meet the epistemic challenge posed by Agrippa's trilemma, among others. The parenthesis in the second premise and the disjunction in the conclusion are introduced so as to include both nihilistic epistemological moral skepticism and Pyrrhonian moral skepticism.[11] With either conclusion, the argument is intended to provide an undercutting defeater for our first-order moral beliefs.[12]

The moral error theorist and the nihilistic epistemological moral skeptic use the disagreement argument to draw a negative conclusion – ontological and epistemological, respectively. In both cases, the kind of negative stance is higher-order, just like the stance adopted by the Academic skeptic and the

---

[11] According to nihilistic epistemological moral skepticism, moral justification (and hence moral knowledge) is impossible. According to Pyrrhonian moral skepticism, our moral beliefs are so far unjustified but moral justification and moral knowledge might be possible.

[12] A similar disagreement argument can be used to target metaethical views by pointing to the (as yet) impossibility of rationally resolving the second-order disputes between them, thereby concluding that they are not (as yet) epistemically justified.

medical Empiricist – and unlike the Pyrrhonist's meta-agnosticism. The moral error theorist affirms that all the conflicting moral judgments are false, which is a first-order claim, but the reason why they are all false is higher-order, namely, that there are no objective moral values, facts, or properties. He also makes the higher-order claim that there is no first-order moral knowledge understood in a robustly realist manner, for there is nothing about which to have such knowledge. The nihilistic epistemological moral skeptic suspends his judgment about any first-order controversial moral claim. In adopting such first-order suspension, he is in line with the Pyrrhonist, the Academic skeptic, and the medical Empiricist. But his ultimate reason for suspending judgment seems to be similar to the reason why the latter two do so: since moral knowledge is impossible or no moral belief is ever epistemically justified, one can never decide whether any of the conflicting moral beliefs, if any, is true. The nihilistic epistemological moral skeptic, too, may be making an inference to the best explanation. Faced with a moral disagreement that he cannot rationally resolve, he suspends his judgment. After finding himself in the same situation with respect to every moral disagreement he encounters, he infers that the best explanation for such unresolvability is that the moral truth, if any there be, cannot be found. Once he gets to this nihilistic second-order view, he acquires stronger grounds for his first-order suspension.[13]

4 Religious Disagreement

Just like moral disagreement, religious disagreement is a phenomenon we regularly encounter in our daily lives. Not only is there the disagreement between the agnostic or the naturalist and the person who believes in the existence of a personal god or an ultimate transcendent reality,[14] but also the countless disputes between the different religions and the many controversies within the same religious traditions. Philosophers of religion have for some time

---

[13] Sarah McGrath (2008) proposes an argument from moral disagreement intended to show that one's belief about a controversial moral matter does not amount to knowledge when one has no more reason to think that the person who denies one's belief is in error than that one is. Her view differs from both nihilistic epistemological moral skepticism and Pyrrhonian moral skepticism in that its target is moral knowledge rather than moral justification. Although these two forms of skepticism also target moral knowledge, McGrath claims neither that it is unreasonable to hold moral beliefs about controversial moral matters of the above kind nor that we should suspend judgment about them. Her view also differs from nihilistic epistemological moral skepticism in that she does not (as far as I can see) claim that we will never be able to attain moral knowledge about the moral matters in question. In this regard, she seems closer to Pyrrhonian moral skepticism.

[14] I refer here to the naturalist rather than the atheist because the latter may deny the existence of a god or gods but accept that there is some sort of ultimate supernatural reality – and also several kinds of supernatural entities. The naturalist, by contrast, claims that there is nothing beyond the natural realm.

now explored whether religious disagreement calls into question the truth or the rationality of religious belief. The discussion of the challenge posed by religious diversity has been conducted mainly within the framework of the debate between exclusivism, pluralism, internalism, and skepticism. The first three positions exhibit each several variants, but it is possible to offer the following brief characterizations of them.[15]

The exclusivist maintains that his religion is entirely true or true regarding the important religious matters, or that his religion comes closer to the truth *tout court* or to the truth concerning the important religious matters, whereas the other religions are entirely or mostly false or considerably deviate from the truth. For this reason, his religion is the only one that offers the means to salvation.

The pluralist affirms that all religions, or at least an important number of them, are epistemically or soteriologically on a par: they are equally true or make it possible to achieve salvation – it is usually thought that the reason why they are all routes to salvation is that they are all equally true. For the sake of plausibility, the pluralist may restrict the scope of his view by saying that his religion as well as others are equally true with respect to their claims about the supreme or ultimate religious reality. He may believe that each of the religions in question offers a partial account of the ultimate reality and that together they provide a complete and accurate account.

The inclusivist adopts a middle position between exclusivism and pluralism, for he claims that, even though his own religion is true in general or regarding the important religious matters and hence those who profess it are in a privileged position with respect to salvation, salvation is not exclusive to them. The reason is either that other religions share some of the true doctrines of his own religion or that those who do not profess his religion have certain virtues or attitudes that make them worthy of salvation.

Despite their differences, the three positions in question agree that (i) there exists a supernatural or transcendent entity or reality to which (ii) we can have some degree of cognitive access. By contrast, the religious skeptic points out that the awareness of the existence of deep, widespread, and persistent inter- and intrareligious disagreements support (a) the denial of the existence of such an entity or reality – and, hence, the denial of its knowability since there is nothing to be known – or (b) the denial of the possibility of moral knowledge or justified moral belief, or (c) the suspension of judgment about whether moral knowledge

---

[15] Exclusivism is defended by, among others, Alston (1988) and Plantinga (1995); pluralism mainly by Hick (1988, 1997, 2004); and inclusivism especially by Kvanvig (2021). For a detailed analysis of these three positions and the problems they face, see McKim (2012: chaps. 2–6).

and justified moral belief are possible. In favor of these three skeptical stances, one can offer disagreement-based arguments that parallel those in favor of the distinct forms of moral skepticism that were examined in the previous section.

Note also that religious skeptics find in the disagreement between exclusivists, pluralists, and inclusivists more grist for their skeptical mill. Not only are there countless religious controversies but also, in their attempt to find an adequate way to cope with them, philosophers of religion fall into a new, second-order disagreement. What is troubling about this disagreement over what to make of religious controversies is that the disputants are fully aware of the challenge posed by such controversies, seem to be smart and intellectually honest truth seekers, have devoted a lot of time and effort to studying the matter, and are familiar with the objections leveled against their respective views.[16]

A serious difficulty encountered when dealing with disagreement among believers or between believers and nonbelievers is that believers usually appeal to their personal experiences of something they characterize as holly or divine or supernatural or transcendent. Note, to begin with, that the notion of personal experience is tricky since the boundary between personal experience and publicly available evidence is sometimes blurred. Let me give you an example. Twenty years ago, I visited some relatives in the city of Concordia, in Argentina. During my visit, I accompanied my cousin to the house of a friend of his where we had a conversation with the latter's mother. While narrating the story of the twenty-meter wooden-sculpted crucified Christ found outside the city, she told us that, one day, when she and three other people were praying at the foot of the wooden Christ, they all witnessed how it started to weep blood. While listening to what sounded as a sincere testimony, I smiled and thought that, if I had been there, I would have seen no tears and no blood. Is this a case of publicly available evidence? I suppose that the group of witnesses would have said so, while at the time I thought that this had been a case of collective hallucination, that is, a hallucination induced, by the power of suggestion, to a group of people who share the same religious beliefs and who are in a heightened emotional state. But suppose that my explanation is wrong, that what they claimed to have seen did occur, and that I would nonetheless have seen nothing had I been there. We could then describe the event as a religious experience shared exclusively by a small group of people who possessed some kind of special capacity to perceive certain events, and so as a case in which the evidence was not publicly available in the sense that it could not be seen by anyone with properly

---

[16] The agnostic (nihilistic or Pyrrhonian) also calls attention to the disagreement between the atheist and the theist, or between the naturalist and the supernaturalist, and to the impossibility (as of yet) to resolve it in a rational manner.

functioning vision. However, it could instead be argued that, even though the evidence was publicly available and could in principle be seen by anyone, in order to do so one had to be open to seeing evidence of that kind.

Note, second, that my reaction at the time was due to the fact that I was (and still am) an agnostic, although a considerable number of Christians (to restrict the discussion to that group) would have reacted in the same way upon hearing the story – most of those to whom I told it said that the four witnesses must have been hallucinating. Let us consider first the disagreement between the two groups of Christians, that is, between those who believe that the wooden Christ did weep blood and those who believe that it did not. How is that disagreement to be explained? Those from the latter group mostly told me that such things do not happen. This opinion is surprising and hasty because it seems to be inconsistent with their religious beliefs, since Christians claim to believe in some really amazing things, such as Jesus's being the son of God, his resurrection, his postresurrection apparitions, or his ascension. Catholics also believe in Marian apparitions and in miracles performed by persons who were declared saints. Given their holding beliefs of that kind, it seems that the Christians under consideration should have said that the specific supernatural event referred to in the wooden Christ story did not occur rather than that events of that kind do not happen at all. But on what grounds could they base their disbelief in the story? Taking into account their entire web of religious beliefs, it seems that a cautious attitude of suspension would be more reasonable. This is so even if they would have seen no tears or blood had they been there, for many Christians believe that people may have private veridical religious experiences.

Let us now consider my own reaction as a nonbeliever. Can I confidently deny the truth of the wooden Christ story? Notice, first, that my being an agnostic does not by itself preclude me from believing that a specific religious story is false, for I may have an undefeated rebutting defeater. For instance, I may know that the testifier has a documented history of psychotic episodes that occurred independently of substance use, or I may know that the testifier sometimes consumes psychedelic drugs and that he often has religious visions when he does so, or I may know that the testifier suffers from mythomania. I did not have such specific rebutting defeaters for the wooden Christ story, and so I appealed to collective hallucination as a reason to disbelieve it. But it seems that I should have been more cautious or humbler. Why? For the same reasons that I cannot rule out the possibility of veridical religious experiences in general. In my own case, one of the main reasons is that there are seemingly intelligent, informed, careful, and intellectually honest people who hold religious beliefs, some of which they claim to be based on their own personal religious experiences. Think of such accomplished and respected Christian philosophers as William Alston, Alvin Plantinga, and Gary Gutting, all of whom defend in their writings the rationality of religious belief. These are philosophers who, with regard to cognitive abilities and access to relevant evidence, are at the very least my epistemic equals, and most probably my epistemic superiors, as far as philosophical matters are concerned. Of course, they are not perfect epistemically speaking, and so they could be mistaken in their religious beliefs. But the same goes for accomplished and respected atheistic and agnostic philosophers. In religious matters, we are faced with various disagreements between philosophers who appear to be roughly equals in their epistemic standing and who put forward arguments that seem to be roughly of equal strength. For this reason, I myself feel constrained to with-hold my assent when it comes to religious matters despite the fact that any kind of religious experience is entirely foreign to me – up till now at least.

A further key point to take into consideration is that whether a given experience is to be judged a hallucination or a veridical religious experience depends on one's background beliefs or one's worldview more generally. For example, the resolution of the disagreement about whether a person's perception as of Virgin Mary is evidence that she is hallucinating or evidence that a genuine Marian apparition is occurring requires, in part, the resolution of other deeper and more complex controversies. Indeed, certain real-life religious disputes are to be explained by fundamental epistemic disagreements between individuals who defend conflicting views on what is a reliable source of information or a reliable method of inquiry: should we trust science, common sense, the Bible, revelation, religious testimony, all of them? Deep disputes between, for example, naturalists and supernaturalists do not seem epistemically resolvable inasmuch as the conflicting basic epistemic principles they endorse cannot be defended, when challenged, by means of noncircular arguments. This is not to say that there is *no* common ground between them that makes communication, debate, and mutual understanding possible, but only that there does not appear to be *enough* common ground on the basis of which rational agreement can be reached. How could we resolve in an impartial way the dispute between, for example, those philosophers who believe in the Biblical God, Jesus's resurrection, and the latter's presence in the Eucharist, and those who regard such beliefs as being as irrational or superstitious as beliefs in astrology, cartomancy, or witchcraft? Given their adoption of what seem to be significantly different worldviews, it seems that any change of mind of one of them will most likely be the result, not of the appreciation of the epistemic reasons provided by his rival, but rather of a fundamental conversion or of a kind of persuasion brought about by his rival's engaging his emotions (cf. Wittgenstein 1969: §§ 262, 609–612; Kuhn 1977: 338, 1996: 150–151, 204; Haidt 2013: 56–58). It appears that some disagreements just cannot be resolved by "knowing the facts" or by "being more rational or intelligent."[17]

How should someone involved in such a disagreement react upon realizing the impossibility of providing noncircular arguments for his view and the extreme difficulty of convincing his opponent, or of being convinced by him, by means of arguments? By my lights, suspension is called for. Otherwise, the Christian philosopher should conclude that he has been lucky enough to find the truth by having a religious experience and having the ability to appreciate its veridicality, while the naturalist philosopher, who appears to be cognitively on a par with him in most respects, is still in the dark due to her lacking either the experience or the ability or both. Likewise, the naturalist philosopher should conclude that she has been lucky enough to have, unlike the Christian philosopher who appears to be cognitively on a par with her in most respects, the ability to recognize the hallucinatory or delusional nature of the Christian philosopher's religious experience or even of her own religious experience if she happened to have one. That suspension is the attitude to be adopted is even clearer in the case of an uninvolved observer who has not yet taken a stand on the matter. For the Christian philosopher and the naturalist philosopher appear to have similar epistemic credentials, they both put forward elaborate arguments in favor of their respective views, and they both are unable to defend their diverging fundamental epistemic principles in a noncircular manner.

It should be emphasized that neither the naturalist nor the agnostic denies that there are religious experiences, that is, that certain persons have experiences as of something that is transcendent or holly or divine. But, as Gutting (1982: 23) remarks, the issue about religious experience is not whether it occurs but whether it is veridical. A nonbeliever with no religious experience is faced with two competing explanations of the religious experiences of others, one religious and another naturalistic and, if he cannot choose between them, he will suspend judgment. But even someone who has had a religious experience may realize that he cannot dismiss a naturalistic explanation of it just as he cannot dismiss a supernaturalistic explanation, and so he may end up suspending judgment. This is so even if the experience is incredibly vivid, clear, and intense, for such phenomenological features of the experience can be given a seemingly plausible naturalistic explanation. It is sometimes claimed that, if after having a religious

---

[17] The points made in this paragraph concern the issue of deep disagreement, which has received renewed attention in recent years but which I cannot address further here for lack of space. For a fine overview, see Ranalli & Thirza (2022a, 2022b).

experience a person undergoes a moral transformation, finds purpose in life, or finds a strength of will he did not have, one can take these changes are evidence that the experience is veridical. However, one can offer a competing and seemingly equally plausible explanation: the changes are actually caused by the emotions and attitudes (joy, gratitude, humility) generated by the experience and by the delusional beliefs in the supernatural entities (a deity or deceased relatives) or the supernatural realm (heaven or an afterworld) that one forms on the basis of the experience.

Last but not least, when addressing the issue of religious experience, we face the problem that believers sometimes have seemingly incompatible religious experiences. For example, some people experience the ultimate transcendent reality as personal while others experience it as impersonal. So, even if we accept that there is such a thing as veridical religious experience, we must find a reliable way to determine which, if any, of the conflicting religious experiences we know of are veridical. A religious pluralist might argue that the very same reality reveals itself in different ways, and so that divergent religious experiences may all be veridical. Setting aside whether this view makes any sense, we face the problem that religious pluralism is rejected by exclusivists and inclusivists, which prompts us to find a reliable way to resolve such a second-order religious disagreement.

I have discussed certain issues concerning religious disagreement mainly because religious controversies are among the most common real-life disputes, which are those whose epistemic implications epistemologists should, by my lights, be most interested in examining. Also, the treatment of disagreement in religious epistemology is the immediate antecedent of the current discussion of disagreement in general epistemology. This is reasonable because some of the leading epistemologists in the 1980s, 1990s, and 2000s were also philosophers of religion or had a strong interest in the philosophy of religion. As has been noted by others, the term "epistemic peer," which plays a key role in the contemporary debate on the epistemic significance of disagreement, was coined by Gutting in his 1982 book-length treatment of the justification of religious belief.[18] Therein, he rejects the view that religious belief is not something for which one needs rational grounds or that demands for a justification of religious belief are inappropriate. One of his reasons for rejecting that view is the existence of disagreements among inquirers who appear to be equally

---

[18] Jonathan Kvanvig (1983) also talks of disagreement among "epistemic peers" about the existence of God, but he does not mention Gutting (1982). In personal communication, he confirmed that he did not get the term from Gutting. Note also that Richard Feldman, one of the early main contributors to the epistemology of disagreement literature, first wrote a short article replying to Alvin Plantinga's self-defeat objection to religious pluralism in which he somewhat anticipates his conciliatory view on disagreement (Feldman 2003). And in his later work on disagreement, religious controversy continues to occupy a prominent place (Feldman 2007, 2021).

intelligent, perspicacious, reasonable, thorough, and honest. The fact that an epistemic peer (an atheist, an agnostic, or another believer) disagrees with one about the religious belief one holds indicates that one needs to provide reasons for holding it; their disagreement poses an epistemic challenge to one's belief that one must try to meet (Gutting 1982: 11–12, 85).

5 The Epistemology of Disagreement

Over the past two decades, the epistemic significance of disagreement has been a hot topic in analytic epistemology.[19] The literature on the epistemology of disagreement has focused primarily on determining which doxastic attitude one is rationally required to adopt upon discovering a disagreement with someone whom on considers an epistemic peer. Discussion of peer disagreement has for the most part centered on two-person disputes, but some authors have also examined multi-person disputes – either between a person and a certain number of his peers or between groups of peers (e.g., Lackey 2013; Christensen 2014).[20]

In what follows, I first briefly explain the notion of epistemic peerhood. I then refer to the debate between conciliationists and steadfasters about how one should rationally react to the discovery of disagreement. Next, I present two views according to which one can legitimately retain one's belief by appealing to the ineliminability of the first-person perspective, the information one possesses about one's own epistemic situation, and the high degree of justified confidence in one's own belief. In so doing, I give some reasons why I find those two views unsatisfying. But my main case against them is based on psychological research that provides evidence that self-knowledge is both limited and inaccurate. After reviewing that research, I argue that the views in question also face the problem that often enough one lacks (full) relevant information about the epistemic standing of one's disputants. Lastly, I briefly discuss a *sui generis* view called "skeptical dogmatism."

---

[19] For in-depth introductions to the epistemology of disagreement, see Frances (2014) and Matheson (2015). For advanced collective volumes, see Feldman & Warfield (2010), Christensen & Lackey (2013), and Machuca (2013).

[20] For reasons of space, I will not examine multi-person disputes and the relevance of numbers. I here merely note three problems to be addressed in dealing with those issues. First, with respect to many controversial matters, it is unclear exactly how many people disagree, and how many agree, with us. Second, the majority view (including the majority view among experts) on controversial matters sometimes (radically) change over time, and it seems that awareness of this fact should make us regard the present majority view on a given matter with some caution. Third, it is widely accepted that when group members form a belief independently of one another, the shared belief carries more epistemic weight than when they influence one another or when they are influenced by a common source. The problem is that it is often difficult to determine whether a given belief belongs to one class or the other – which is further complicated by the fact that one's belief about a controversial matter is typically based on other beliefs, some of which may have been independently formed and some of which may have not.

5.1 Epistemic Peerhood

As we saw at the end of Section 4, Gutting (1982) understands the notion of epistemic peerhood solely in terms of cognitive parity. He thinks this is enough to raise an epistemic challenge to one's belief about a disputed matter. Kvanvig understands it in the same way, but he remarks that, since epistemic peerhood only means equality with respect to intellectual virtues but not with respect to the possession of relevant evidence or of reliable methods for acquiring evidence, the mere fact that an epistemic peer disagrees with one does not give one a reason to question one's belief (Kvanvig 1983: 53–54 and n. 17).

The fact that such a conception of epistemic peerhood is less threatening to the epistemic credentials of one's beliefs about controversial matters explains why, in current epistemological discussions of peer disagreement, epistemic peerhood is typically understood in terms of both *cognitive* and *evidential parity*. Thus, two individuals are epistemic peers with regard to the question whether *p* if and only if (i) they are equally intelligent, perspicacious, reasonable, thorough, and unbiased, and (ii) they are equally familiar with the available evidence relevant to the question whether *p* (evidence including data that directly bears on the question, background knowledge, and arguments for and against the conflicting views on whether *p*). Evidential parity is reached after *full disclosure*, that is, after the disputants have completely shared with each other their reasons for their respective beliefs about whether *p*.

There is, though, another conception of epistemic peerhood to be found in the peer disagreement literature: two individuals are epistemic peers with regard to a given question if and only if they are, prior to the disagreement, equally likely to be right about that question. It could be argued, however, that one's assessment of such antecedent likelihood depends on one's assessment of both the disputants' cognitive abilities and their familiarity with the relevant evidence.

One problem with the conception of epistemic peerhood in terms of perfect cognitive and evidential equality is that it is idealized, and so that it cannot be applied to real-life disagreements. From a more realistic point of view, two individuals are epistemic peers with regard to a given question if and only if (i) they possess similar cognitive abilities, and (ii) they are familiar with the available evidence bearing on that question to roughly the same degree.

5.2 Conciliationism vs Steadfastness

Two main views have been defended in the literature on the epistemic significance of peer disagreement, which are commonly labeled "conciliationist" and "steadfast." In this section, I offer a rough characterization of them and their most important varieties.

Conciliationism maintains that all the parties to an acknowledged peer dispute are rationally required to significantly revise their beliefs because of the epistemic symmetry between them. Thus, upon learning that a peer disagrees with one about whether p, one cannot rationally continue to believe that p or to hold the belief that p with a high degree of confidence.[21] According to the conciliationist, discovering a peer disagreement makes one wonder whether one has not made a mistake in evaluating the available evidence bearing on whether p. For example, if I am a doctor who diagnose a patient with a given disease based on his symptoms and the results of various tests but then discover that a colleague whom I consider my epistemic equal has reached a different diagnosis after evaluating the same data, I gain a reason to think that I have incorrectly evaluated the evidence – and so does my colleague if he considers me his epistemic equal. The defeater provided by peer disagreement may be rebutting if one thinks that one must conciliate to the point of adopting one's opponent belief, or undercutting if one thinks that one must conciliate only to the point of suspending judgment about which of the competing beliefs, if any, is true.

The most prominent conciliationist position is what Adam Elga calls the "Equal Weight View":

> *Equal Weight View (EWV)*
> It is rationally required to give equal weight to the beliefs of both parties to a peer disagreement when there is no reason to prefer one belief to the other that is independent of the disagreement itself.[22]

This view can be interpreted in two different ways depending on whether one adopts a coarse- or a fine-grained approach to doxastic attitudes. On the former approach, the disputants must suspend judgment about whether p when they learn of the peer disagreement, since there are only three possible doxastic attitudes that may be adopted, namely, belief, disbelief, and suspension. On the latter approach, the disputants must split the difference in the degrees of confidence in their respective beliefs.[23]

---

[21] Various forms of conciliationism are embraced by, e.g., Feldman (2003, 2006, 2007), Christensen (2007, 2011, 2013), Elga (2007, 2010), Kornblith (2010, 2013), and Matheson (2015).

[22] For Elga's own formulation of the EWV, see Elga (2007: 490). This view is already found in Sidgwick (1895: 152–153, 1905: 464); cf. Sidgwick (1874: 321).

[23] One of the most serious charges leveled particularly against the EWV is the self-defeat objection: if the proponent of the EWV finds out that an epistemic peer believes the EWV to be false, then he should give to this belief the same weight as he gives to his own belief in the truth of the EWV and, hence, either suspend judgment about its truth or split the difference in the degrees of confidence with which he and his opponent hold their respective beliefs. The EWV is therefore self-defeating because, in order to propose it as the rationally required response to peer disagreement, its proponent must be confident that it is true, in which case he is nonetheless required to significantly lower his confidence in its truth inasmuch as he knows that there is an epistemic peer who rejects it. The advocate of the EWV is thus rationally bound by the EWV

The above version of the EWV refers to a requirement, commonly called "Independence," which might be formulated thus:

Independence
In order to resolve a peer disagreement, neither disputant may rely on reasons that are not independent of both his initial belief about the disputed matter and the reasoning behind that belief.[24]

What conciliationists seek to avoid with this principle is any dogmatic or bootstrapping move by means of which one could dismiss out of hand one's peer's dissenting opinion simply because it is different from one's own. Some have rejected Independence on the grounds that, in many cases, one's peer's disagreement over a given question shows that he has not responded appropriately to the first-order evidence bearing on that question.[25] This is so when, for example, my peer disagrees with me about whether $12 \times 5 = 60$ or about whether there is a person sitting two feet in front of us. In these cases, it is argued, I begin with an extremely high level of justified confidence in the truth of my belief and the reliability of my faculties, and it is therefore absolutely clear that my peer is suffering from some kind cognitive malfunctioning or else being insincere. One may reply, however, that such cases can be accounted for without appeal to the belief about the disputed issue or the reasoning behind it, but to more general considerations. For it could be argued that, since it is highly unlikely that two persons thinking lucidly about the kinds of issues in question hold contrary opinions, the most probable explanation of their disagreement is that one of them is confused, disingenuous, or cognitively deficient (see Christensen 2007: 198–201, 2011: 8–12).

Another key thesis endorsed by at least the great majority of conciliationists is the so-called "Uniqueness Thesis":

Uniqueness Thesis (UT)
The total available evidence E bearing on proposition p rationally justifies only one doxastic attitude towards p or one degree of confidence in p.[26]

This thesis claims that, given E, there is a unique doxastic attitude towards p that it is fully rational to adopt or a unique level of credence in p that it is fully

---

itself to lose confidence in it. For reasons of space, I cannot review the various replies to the objection found in the literature, but see Machuca (2022: chap. 9) and the references therein.

[24] Somewhat similar versions of this principle are endorsed by, e.g., Christensen (2007), Elga (2007), and Kornblith (2010). On the difficulties in formulating Independence, see Moon (2018) and Christensen (2019).

[25] For arguments against Independence, see Enoch (2010), Sosa (2010), Kelly (2013), and Lord (2014).

[26] Proponents of UT include Christensen (2007), Feldman (2007), and Matheson (2011). Detractors include Douven (2009), Conee (2010), Kelly (2010), and Ballantyne & Coffman (2011, 2012).

rational to possess.[27] It is plain why this thesis is endorsed by at least most conciliationists: the reason why, in the face of peer disagreement, one is rationally required to abandon one's belief is that at most one of the beliefs held by the disputants may be right. If conflicting beliefs about the same matter were supported by the same evidence and the disputants were therefore fully rational in their beliefs, then there would be no need for them to revise their beliefs.

Those who reject UT endorse epistemic permissivism, which might be formulated thus:

Permissivism
Given the total available evidence E bearing on p, different doxastic attitudes towards p, or different degrees of confidence in p, are equally rational.[28]

According to the permissivist, there are some cases in which the evidence supports conflicting beliefs, so that each of the disputants is rational to hold the belief he or she holds. In those cases, the evidence may be depicted as complex and ambiguous. If so, is it really rationally permissible for different persons to hold conflicting beliefs once they acknowledge the disagreement between them and the complexity and ambiguity of the evidence? Permissivism can be interpreted in terms of there being *equally strong* evidence in favor of conflicting beliefs about p, or in terms of conflicting beliefs about p being *underdetermined* by the total available evidence. If so, it seems that the permissivist should recognize *malgré lui* that the evidential situation is such that suspension is the rationally required response to the disagreement over p. From the external vantage point of someone who has not formed any belief about the matter and is looking for answers, it seems arbitrary to defend any single view: why would he prefer one view to any other when he is aware that they are all (supposedly) equally well supported by the same body of evidence? The only rationally required attitude for him to adopt appears to be suspension. And from the vantage point of the disputants themselves, it seems that, if they become aware that the evidence is complex and ambiguous, they should conclude that they cannot actually rationally stick to their guns, but should instead suspend judgment. Otherwise, they would suffer from a doxastic tension: on the one hand, they would believe that the views of their dissenters are equally well supported by the available evidence, but, on the other, they would believe that

---

[27] In the rest of this paragraph, I will talk in terms of the coarse-grained approach to doxastic attitudes.

[28] For defenses of permissivism, see especially Kelly (2014) and Schoenfield (2014, 2019). For criticism of that view, see White (2005, 2014). Christensen (2007: 211, 2009: 763–764) and Ballantyne and Coffman (2012) argue that some permissive accounts of rational belief are compatible with conciliationism.

their own assessment of the evidence is correct. Their own view might actually be true: if a new piece of evidence were found, we would perhaps realize that the new body of evidence supports only one of the conflicting views, or that it supports one of them more than it supports the others. But in the current evidential situation any choice between the conflicting views seems capricious.[29] The same line of thought applies if it were argued that, on the basis of the same evidence, conflicting beliefs about p are rational because the disputants have different epistemic standards or prior probability distributions or cognitive goals (Kelly 2014; Schoenfield 2014). For if the disputants become aware of this fact and cannot affirm that one epistemic standard or probability distribution or cognitive goal is epistemically to be preferred to the others, should they not suspend judgment about whether p? Alternatively, if one is epistemically to be preferred to the others, then, even though some beliefs about p are reasonably held in the sense that they are required by the mistaken epistemic standards or probability distributions or cognitive goals, only one belief about whether p is strictly rational.

Conciliationism is rejected by steadfasters, who maintain that peer disagreement does not always provide a reason for the disputants to revise their beliefs, since in at least some cases it is perfectly reasonable to retain one's belief with the same degree of confidence.[30] While some steadfasters maintain that only one of the parties to a peer disagreement can reasonably retain his belief, others maintain that both parties can do so.[31] This difference depends on whether the reasonableness of the belief is understood in terms of which of the competing beliefs is best supported by the shared first-order evidence, or rather in terms of whether from a first-person perspective each of the disputants has legitimate reasons for preferring his own belief to his rival's.[32] All steadfasters reject Independence, since they maintain that a person can prefer his own belief to that of his rival by appealing to the fact of the disagreement itself – as the mathematical and perception cases referred to above show.

Some views on the epistemic significance of peer disagreement occupy a middle ground between conciliationism and steadfastness. Such is the case of the Total Evidence View (Kelly 2010). In line with steadfastness, that view maintains that, in evaluating how one should react to the discovery of a disagreeing peer, one should take into account not only the higher-order evidence (i.e., each disputant's opinion)

---

[29] The point made in this paragraph is of course related to the arbitrariness objection to permissivism.

[30] Steadfast positions are defended by, e.g., van Inwagen (1996, 2010), Kelly (2005), Wedgwood (2007, 2010), Sosa (2010), Weatherson (2013, 2019), and Schafer (2015).

[31] Wedgwood (2007), Sosa (2010), and Schafer (2015) claim that both disputants can reasonably hold their ground, while Kelly (2005) maintains that only one of them can do so.

[32] As far as I can tell, Kelly (2005) understands reasonableness in the first sense, whereas Wedgwood (2007) and Sosa (2010) understand it in the second.

but also the first-order evidence (i.e., the evidence directly pertaining to the disputed issue). In some cases, one can reasonably privilege one's own belief over that of one's peer, namely, when one has correctly evaluated the original, first-order evidence. However, in line with conciliationism, the Total Evidence View claims that one should always give at least some small weight to one's peer belief, and hence that one's confidence in one's own belief should always be at least slightly diminished when confronted with a disagreeing peer, even if one has responded appropriately to the first-order evidence.

5.3 First-Person Perspective, Self-Trust, and Personal Information

This section discusses two related views that can be regarded as versions of steadfastness inasmuch as they (a) maintain that one can sometimes rationally retain one's belief in the face of peer disagreement and (b) deny that one should always give at least some small weight to one's peer's belief. The first view appeals to the ineliminability of the first-person perspective and the self-trust that comes with it.[33] The second appeals to the asymmetry between the information one possesses about one's own epistemic situation and the information one possesses about one's rival's epistemic situation, and to the high level of justified confidence in the correctness of one's belief about the disputed issue.[34]

It is plain that the first-person perspective cannot be completely eliminated. When engaged in a disagreement with someone, it is I who judge whether that person is my epistemic peer, superior, or inferior, or it is I who judge that I am (currently) unable to determine what that person's epistemic standing is in relation to mine. Hence, it is I who determine whether I am rationally required to revise my belief about the disputed matter and, if so, to what extent. Even if I adopt a third-person perspective to analyze the epistemic implications of the disagreement, the first-person perspective cannot be entirely eliminated, since the analysis is ultimately conducted from a first-person vantage point: it is I who determine how the disagreement would look from an allegedly neutral vantage point. In each case, I trust the results of my deliberations, and so there seems to be an inescapable degree of trust in my own opinions and assessments.

Given the ineliminability of the first-person perspective and the self-trust that comes with it, it seems that, when I believe that *p*, I can legitimately take my

---

[33] Different versions of this view are defended by Foley (2001: 79, 108–112), Enoch (2010), Wedgwood (2010), Pasnau (2015), and Schafer (2015). I will here focus on the view as defended by Enoch.

[34] This view is defended particularly by Lackey (2010) and Sosa (2010), and so my discussion below focuses on their positions. But see also Christensen (2009: 759–760, 2011: 9–10), Frances (2010: 441–442), and Matheson (2015: 103–104, 118, 121–122).

opponent's belief that not-p as evidence that he is mistaken and, hence, that he is less reliable than I am with respect to the topic at hand. From my own first-person vantage point, my reason for doing so is not that he believes not-p whereas I believe p, but rather that he believes not-p whereas p (Enoch 2010: 982). That is, the reason is not that his belief is different from mine, but rather that it is false (as I believe). Thus, at least sometimes I may legitimately take the disagreement itself as a reason to demote my opponent from peerhood (Enoch 2010: 979–981).

Note, first, that the above line of argument begs the question against my peer, and in a problematic way (*contra* Enoch 2010: 980–981). For the subject of our dispute is precisely whether *that p* or *that not-p*. That is, we engage in a dialectical exchange in order to determine which is true: my belief that p or rather his belief that not-p. In such a context, it does not seem legitimate to simply take for granted *that p*.

Second, an uninvolved observer would remark that, just as I can take *that p* (as I believe) as evidence against my opponent's reliability, so too can my opponent take *that not-p* (as he believes) as evidence against my reliability. Thus, from the vantage point of an uninvolved observer, the disagreement cannot be resolved because there is a dialectical symmetry between the disputants. But even from my own vantage point, once I become aware that my opponent demotes me because *that not-p* (as he believes), I may wonder whether I am really entitled to demote him because *that p* (as I believe). It may be argued that the symmetry I am committed to is that between my view and my rival's, not between p and not-p (insofar as I believe p), and so my reason for demoting my rival (i.e., *that p*) is not a reason I have for demoting myself (Enoch 2010: 982, 985, 987). But, once again, my opponent can reason in exactly the same way, something of which I am fully aware. The key point is that, from my own first-person perspective, I am aware both of the symmetry resulting from the fact that both my rival and I appeal to self-trust in an attempt to show that one is entitled to stick to one's own belief in the face of disagreement, and of the fact that I regard my rival's belief as false despite his relying on self-trust. I thus become aware that self-trust is no guarantee that one's beliefs about controversial issues are true: if at most one of us may be correct, then self-trust does not prevent at least one of us from getting things wrong. The crucial question then is: what is so special about me that, unlike my rival, I cannot be mistaken in my belief despite relying on self-trust?

There seems to be a dialectical symmetry between my rival and me that has epistemic implications, the kind of symmetry that calls for suspension and that can be appreciated from a first-person point of view. Even though I am unable to eliminate entirely the first-person perspective, I am still able, from my own vantage point, to call into question self-trust as a reliable source of knowledge or justification. Ineliminability entails neither infallibility nor reliability: the fact that we cannot but use our cognitive faculties when inquiring does not entail that these faculties are either infallible or reliable, or that they are less fallible or more reliable than the cognitive faculties of our opponents. Hence, even if the first-person perspective is ineliminable, this ineliminability does not prevent one from subjecting one's own beliefs about controversial matters to rigorous criticism, and so one can refrain from endorsing the verdicts of one's cognitive capacities on those matters.

The second view to be considered maintains that the abundant and accurate information one has about one's own mental states and the normal functioning of one's own cognitive capacities enables one to avoid engaging in doxastic revision in many cases of real-life disagreement. Such information functions as a symmetry breaker because one lacks the same kind of information about the epistemic situation of one's opponent. One can therefore legitimately hold one's ground and dismiss one's opponent's opinion inasmuch as one has a high degree of justified confidence in the veridicality of one's own phenomenology and the reliability of one's own cognitive capacities.

Let us consider three examples given in support of that view. First, suppose that I ask my boss if I can leave early from work because I have a headache. In this case, I know full well that I have a headache – in this case, I cannot be mistaken about my ongoing conscious experience – even if my boss claims that I am faking it. In a case like this, the principle of Independence cannot properly be applied because it is legitimate to downgrade one's opponent's ability to correctly assess the evidence by appealing to the substance of the disagreement (Sosa 2010: 286). Second, suppose that I affirm but my roommate denies that a mutual friend is eating lunch with us at the dining room table in our apartment. In such a situation, not only does it clearly seem to me that my friend is sitting at the table, but I also know that I have never in my life hallucinated an object, that I have not been drinking or taking drugs, that I have my contact lenses in, and that my eyesight functions reliably when my short-nearsightedness is corrected (Lackey 2010: 306–307). Third, suppose that I disagree with a long-time neighbor about the location of a restaurant the two of us frequent. Although prior to the disagreement neither of us had any reason to suspect that the other's memory was in any way deficient and we viewed each other as epistemic peers regarding knowledge of the city, I can retain my belief about the restaurant's location with the same high degree of justified confidence I had before the disagreement occurred. The reason is that I have lived in the city for many years, I know the city extremely well, I have eaten at the restaurant many times, I have not been drinking or taking drugs, and I have ample evidence that my memory is functioning reliably (Lackey 2010: 308–309).

In disagreements like the three just described, I have introspective access to my current phenomenologically vivid experience or I have knowledge about the past and present normal functioning of my cognitive faculties. As a result, even if prior to the disagreement I had good reason to regard my disputants as epistemic peers, it is rational for me to stick to my beliefs. Also, given the extraordinarily high degree of justified confidence with which I hold those beliefs, the fact that my disputants disagree with me is best taken as evidence that they do not have access to relevant information or that something has gone wrong with them – they may be confused because they have been drinking, or they may be hallucinating because they have taken drugs, or they may be suffering from some kind of memory loss.

In reply, notice, to begin with, that it is far from clear that we are entitled to regard ourselves as reliable judges of our own stream of conscious experience, even in circumstances we consider normal or regarding mental states we deem transparent. Eric Schwitzgebel (2011) offers persuasive and empirically informed arguments to the effect that we often err or are confused about our ongoing conscious experience. For example, we do not know whether we dream in color or black-and-white; we are not accurate judges of our visual experience of depth, our eyes-closed visual experience, our visual imagery, or our auditory experience of echolocation; we are in the dark regarding whether we see things double or single and whether consciousness is abundant or sparse; we are prone to go wrong in judging our ongoing emotional phenomenology; and we are at a loss as to whether there is a distinctive phenomenology of thinking. Now, if often enough we do not have reliable introspective access to our ongoing conscious experience, then it seems that we cannot appeal to the phenomenal given or to our current phenomenology as solid rock upon which we can construct a case for remaining steadfast in the face of certain kinds of disagreement.

Second, in the last two disagreements described above, both disputants can offer the same reasons for privileging their own beliefs over those of their rivals. From the vantage point of an external observer who cannot form an opinion on the disputed matters unless the parties reach consensus, neither disagreement can be resolved because both disputants claim to be highly and justifiably confident that their cognitive capacities are reliable and that their performance is accurate. But even from a first-person perspective, it seems that I should suspend judgment. For if I dismiss my rival's opinion because I am not equally confident in the reliability of his cognitive capacities and the accuracy of his performance as I am in the reliability of my own capacities and the accuracy of my own performance, I then learn that he dismisses my opinion for the same reason, and I believe that at most one of us can be right, what is so special about me that I can simply rule out the possibility that it is my confidence that is unjustified? If my rival can be wrong despite his high level of confidence and his reliance on his own personal information, why can I not be wrong despite my high level of confidence and my reliance on my own personal information? If I can entertain the possibility that my disputant is hallucinating or suffering from some kind of memory loss, why can I not entertain the same possibility about myself? Both our own experience and the psychological literature teach us that people suffering from delusion or mnemonic confabulation are unaware of it. This is precisely what happens in the perception and the restaurant cases, since my rival is highly confident in his belief about the absence of our friend at the dining room table or in his belief about the location of the restaurant, even though I think that there is definitely something wrong with him. If I can entertain the possibility that something has gone awry with my opponent without his being aware of it, why can I not entertain the same possibility about myself? For example, how can I know that I have never hallucinated? Have I checked every auditory and visual perception I have ever had against someone else's perception or against a sound or visual recording? If I am one of the many religious believers who have had visions or auditions, should I regard them as veridical or hallucinatory?

In the cases under consideration, there seems to be a dialectical-cum-epistemic symmetry between the disputants: learning that the strategy one's rival follows for resolving the disagreement from his own first-person perspective is the very same strategy one follows for resolving the disagreement from one's own first-person perspective should make one wonder whether the strategy in question is as reliable as one thinks it is. One finds further reasons to call into question such a strategy if, in one's analysis of the disagreement from a first-person vantage point, one incorporates as well experimental evidence to the effect that we do not actually know much about the causes of our beliefs, choices, and behavior – an issue that will be tackled in Section 5.4. It thus seems that, in examining a controversial issue, to one's first-order evidence about it, one should add the higher-order evidence consisting in the fact of the disagreement, the dialectical-cum-epistemic symmetry between the disputants, and the empirical findings provided by experimental research.

Before moving on, let me say something about Lackey's notion of high degree of justified confidence in one's own belief. The first thing to point out is that both parties may have a high degree of confidence in their respective beliefs, and so one must find a reliable way to determine which party is in fact justified in having such a degree of confidence. Here Lackey goes externalist. Regarding the perception case, she invites us to suppose that my roommate denies the presence of our mutual friend at the table because he is hallucinating, and that his hallucination is caused by the fact that, unbeknownst to him, he was drugged by someone. My roommate cannot realize that he is hallucinating because the drug produces no discernible signs. Lackey then argues that although she is happy to grant that, from a purely subjective point of view, my roommate is as reasonable in his belief as I am in mine, our beliefs are not equally justified inasmuch as they are produced by processes that are not equally reliable: in my case the belief is the result of a veridical perceptual experience, while in my roommate's case the belief is the result of a hallucination (Lackey 2010: 320).

I find Lackey's line of argument unsatisfying because, even if from the vantage point of an external observer who is fully informed about the epistemic standing of both disputants it is possible to determine which of the conflicting beliefs was produced by a generally reliable process that is functioning properly, this is much more difficult from the vantage point of the disputants themselves. I may claim that my belief was caused by a properly functioning reliable mechanism, but so too may my opponent. In order to legitimately affirm that he is hallucinating while my belief is based on a veridical perceptual experience, I need to offer, not only to my disputant but also to myself, reasons to claim that I am not the one who has unknowingly taken a drug that produces no noticeable signs.[35] To have such reasons, I need to have some sort of access to the cognitive processes that generate my belief. Thus, if disagreement poses an epistemic challenge the disputants need to meet in a way they regard as responsible and nonarbitrary, then externalism does not seem to be up to the task. Note also that some externalists concede that one fails to have justification or knowledge if one has a believed undefeated defeater (e.g., Goldman 1986: 62–63, 110–112; Plantinga 1993: 40–42; Bergmann 2006: 153–177). Acknowledged disagreement, particularly with someone whom, prior to the disagreement, one has no reason to regard as cognitively deficient, yields a defeater. The only way to defeat that defeater is to offer compelling reasons for the belief that one has correctly evaluated the available evidence because one's cognitive capacities are generally reliable and are functioning properly in the present circumstances. As we will see in the next section, experimental research provides us with additional defeaters inasmuch as it gives us reasons to think that cognitive capacities such as introspection and memory are much less reliable than we take them to be.

---

[35] Someone might object that I fail to differentiate between epistemic justification and dialectical effectiveness. In reply, note that at least certain types of disagreement raise a challenge to search for, and articulate, the actual reasons for one's beliefs. And this not only with the aim of showing to one's disputant that one's belief is well grounded or of convincing him to abandon his belief, but mainly with the aim of determining whether one's own belief is based on rationally grounded considerations or is rather the result of the influence of epistemically contaminating factors. More on this in Section 5.4.

5.4 Incomplete and Misleading Information about Oneself

Over the past fifteen years, several authors have examined the philosophical implications of studies in cognitive psychology that reveal the limits of introspection and the influence of epistemically irrelevant factors on our beliefs. But few authors have examined the relevance of such studies to the question of how one should react to the discovery of disagreement (Ballantyne 2019: chap. 5; Kelly 2022: chap. 10; Machuca 2022: chap. 8). By my lights, their relevance is seen particularly in relation to the strategies for resolving disagreements that were examined in Section 5.3. For those studies seem to force us to recognize, from a first-person perspective, that our self-knowledge is much more limited than we think and, hence, that it is doubtful that we can often rely on personal information to determine which of the disputants (we or our dissenter) is in a better epistemic position *vis-à-vis* the contested issue. In what follows, I review the results of some experimental studies on cognitive overestimation, confabulation, the bias blind spot, confirmation bias, and noise.[36]

5.4.1 Cognitive Overconfidence

People are not in general very good at assessing their own cognitive capacities and performance. The results of a number of experimental studies indicate that we often either overestimate or underestimate our general cognitive competence and our performance in specific circumstances. In a famous article, Justin Kruger and David Dunning (1999) showed that individuals whom they define as "unskilled" or "incompetent" grossly overestimated their overall abilities and test performance both relative to their peers and, to a lesser degree, along absolute performance measures, and that they were unaware that they had performed poorly. These individuals suffer a dual burden, since not only do they reach erroneous conclusions and make poor choices, but their incompetence deprives them of the metacognitive ability to recognize the low quality of their performance. Given their difficulty in recognizing competence not only in themselves but also in others, they are unable to take advantage of the feedback provided by social comparison: they are unable to use information about the superior performance of others to gain insight into the true level of their own performance and then revise their view of their own competence by comparison. Although their aim was to study the overestimation of one's cognitive abilities and performance, Kruger and Dunning found along the way that skilled individuals underestimated their cognitive abilities and test performance relative to their peers. However, since top performers have the metacognitive ability to

---

[36] Sections 5.4.1, 5.4.2, and 5.4.3 partially draw on Machuca (2022: chap. 8).

recognize competence in themselves and others, they are able to use information about the inferior performance of others to raise their estimates of their own performance.

In a subsequent study, Kruger, Dunning, and their colleagues replicated most of the above results by focusing, not only on tasks designed by experimenters, but also on real-world tasks that people encounter in their everyday life: they asked undergraduate students to estimate their performance in course exams, members of college debate teams to estimate their tournament performance, and gun owners attending a competition at a gun club to estimate their performance regarding their knowledge of gun safety and usage (Ehrlinger *et al.* 2008). Other studies have replicated the results among medical lab technicians assessing their knowledge of medical terminology and their problem-solving ability (Haun *et al.* 2000), family medicine residents evaluating their patient-interviewing skills (Hodges *et al.* 2001), medical students assessing their performance on an obstetrics and gynecology clerkship (Edwards *et al.* 2003), undergraduate students evaluating their knowledge of general chemistry (Bell & Volckmann 2011), and graduate students assessing their levels of racial- and gender-based egalitarianism (West & Eaton 2019).

Given those findings, when appealing to personal information to resolve a disagreement, one cannot exclude either the possibility that one will ascribe to oneself cognitive abilities that one does not actually possess, or the possibility that one will believe one has had a performance in evaluating the disputed matter that one has not actually had. It might be argued that, if one is among the skilled, one will first underestimate one's cognitive abilities and performance, but will then be able to correct one's mistaken estimates. It might also be argued that, if one is not among the skilled, one can rely on them when it comes to settling disputes. This is what we do, on a daily basis, when we rely on those whom we regard as experts. Unfortunately, things are actually more complicated, for three reasons.

First, in real life, it is not always easy to determine whether one is among the skilled, for one hardly ever has enough accurate information about one's own track record of success and failure with respect to the countless matters about which one holds opinions. For example, given that confirmation bias is such a widespread phenomenon (more on this in Section 5.3.4), it may occur that one only registers one's track record of success and ignores one's track record of failure. And neither does one usually have enough accurate information about others' (including one's opponents') track record of success and failure so as to be able to compare it with one's own.

Second, it is extremely difficult to determine who – if anyone – is an expert in areas such as religion, morality, politics, and philosophy, in which are found the disputes over most of the matters we care and worry deeply about. Moreover, even in areas such as medicine, it is not always clear-cut who is an expert, for millions of people trust practitioners of alternative medical therapies because they believe that the latter have a proven track record of success – they claim that their own positive experience as patients is compelling evidence of the expertise of alternative medicine practitioners.[37]

Third, experts (whoever they are) in most domains disagree among themselves, and assuming that they cannot all be right, it seems that most of them have actually overestimated their cognitive abilities or their performance in assessing the matters under dispute, and are unaware of their inaccurate estimation.

5.4.2 Confabulation

According to William Hirstein, a subject, S, confabulates if and only if:

1. S claims that p.
2. S believes that p.
3. S's thought that p is ill-grounded.
4. S does not know that her thought is ill-grounded.
5. S should know that her thought is ill-grounded.
6. S is confident that p. (Hirstein 2005: 186).

Chronic confabulation can be produced by different mental disorders: Korsakoff's syndrome, anosognosia for hemiplegia, Capgras delusion, asomatognosia, or Anton's syndrome, among others (see Schnider 2018). But what is intriguing about confabulation is that it often affects mentally healthy people. Young children, subjects of hypnosis, eyewitnesses, or individuals asked to justify their judgments or choices or to describe their mental states may confabulate. The difference between mentally healthy people and clinical patients regarding both the production of false responses and the lack of self-monitoring is actually a matter of degree. As Hirstein points out, what we see in patients is "an extreme version of some basic feature of the human mind, having to do with the way we form beliefs and report them to others" (2005: ix). And as Thalia Wheatley emphasizes, confabulation is an everyday phenomenon:

> [A] wealth of evidence suggests that the healthy brain is far from veridical. In its attempt to create a coherent and predicable world, even basic cognitive processes such as perception and memory are actively constructed, manipulated and embellished, often without our awareness. … [F]iction may be the creation of every *human* mind, not only diseased ones. (2009: 203, italics in the original.)

---

[37] For other considerations about the difficulty for novices to reliably detect expertise, see Ballantyne (2019: 234–241).

Let us first focus on mnemonic confabulation. In a now classic book that shows that eyewitness testimony is much less reliable than we think, Elizabeth Loftus (1979) conceives of it as a three-stage process – the acquisition stage, the retention stage, and the retrieval stage – and explains how each of the stages can be affected by various factors that have distorting effects on a person's testimony by rendering his memories highly inaccurate without his being aware of it. Over the past three decades, there has been a wealth of research on the implantation of entirely false memories of past events or actions through various memory-planting procedures such as hypnosis, pressure to recall, and imagination inflation, as well as on memory distortion caused in a person by the biased way this person retells an event. False memories are a kind of confabulation because the person who has a false memory claims to remember something that either did not happen at all or did not happen in the way he claims it did. When a memory of something – a big or small detail or an entire event – that did not exist is created, it can be as real or vivid to the person as a memory resulting from his perceptions, so that it is extremely difficult to discriminate between them from a first-person perspective. For present purposes, a key point is that nonclinical individuals can produce mnemonic confabulations, which are "a byproduct of normally functioning memory processes and mechanisms, rather than the result of pathological conditions. False memories are completely normal and frequent in everyday life" (French *et al.* 2009: 34).

If mnemonic confabulation is such a common phenomenon, then it is naïve to expect that, for example, a disagreement between two eyewitnesses may be resolved from a first-person perspective by appealing to the information one has about the normal functioning of one's memory. For our memory may well be functioning normally, but what we take to be its normal functioning does not appear to correspond to what its normal functioning actually is: we take a normally functioning memory to be a reliable recorder of what actually happened, when in reality what we remember is a construction or a reconstruction. The epistemic relevance of mnemonic confabulation lies in the fact that to retrieve much of our evidence, including our evidence on controversial matters, we rely on the operation of memory.

The phenomenon of confabulation has also been a focus of attention in studies that examine the influence of intuitions and emotions on moral judgments and voting decisions. Regarding the former, some moral psychologists have called into question the rationalist view according to which moral judgment is caused by a process of conscious reasoning or reflection, claiming instead that it is primarily and directly caused by moral intuitions and emotions (Haidt 2001, 2013). Several studies have shown that induced feelings of disgust unconsciously influence moral judgments by making them harsher, or that they lead people to make negative moral judgments about certain acts even though these acts represent no moral transgression (Wheatley & Haidt 2005; Schnall *et al.* 2008; Horberg *et al.* 2009; Eskine *et al.* 2011). In the latter case, the subjects were puzzled by their negative evaluation, or desperately searched for some kind of justification unrelated to the story, or claimed that, despite not knowing why, the act was just wrong. On the basis of such studies, it has been argued that moral reasoning is usually nothing but an *ex post facto* process by means of which one seeks arguments that will justify an already-made judgment with the aim of influencing the intuitions and actions of others (Haidt 2001: 814, 818, 2013: xx–xxi).

If that theory of moral judgment is correct, two interrelated points are worth making. First, it seems that moral disagreements are to be explained, at least to a considerable extent, by the different emotions experienced by the disputants rather than by their making reason-based judgments. Second, we have limited self-knowledge inasmuch as most of us are unaware of the significant influence that emotions exert on our moral judgments and usually "fabricate" arguments with the aim of justifying those judgments. Note that even someone who is aware of that influence may be unable to determine the extent to which at present a moral judgment of his is under such an influence, and whether the reasons he offers in its support are merely rationalizations. It therefore seems unrealistic to expect that, when involved in a real-life moral disagreement, one may resolve it by having recourse to the information one possesses about the reasons for one's moral view or about the normal functioning of one's cognitive capacities.

As regards voting decisions, we usually think that they are based mainly on rational and careful considerations, such as the candidate's position on issues the voter considers important. However, several studies have shown that voting decisions are, to a considerable extent, influenced by epistemically irrelevant factors – such as the facial appearance of candidates or the location where people are assigned to vote – without the voters being aware of such an influence (Todorov *et al.* 2005; Ballew & Todorov 2007; Berger *et al.* 2008; Olivola & Todorov 2010). Those studies appear to provide strong evidence that often enough we confabulate when explaining the reasons why we chose a given candidate or supported a given initiative inasmuch as those were not the actual reasons for our decisions. If so, then we seem to have grounds for thinking that in the case of political disagreements, too, it might be naïve to expect that one can privilege one's view over the view of one's rival by relying on the supposedly accurate information one has about one's own epistemic standing.

Confabulation is a clear example of failure of self-knowledge: we confabulate not only about the reasons for decisions that may be considered trivial, but also about our personal histories and our moral and political beliefs or choices, which we take to reveal who we are. If we accept the results of the experimental studies that have been reviewed, it seems that we should conclude that the frequent occurrence of the phenomenon of confabulation poses a serious challenge to the appeal to personal information as a reliable strategy for settling disputes from a first-person perspective. For it seems that, more often than we think, the narratives we tell about the reasons for our decisions, choices, or beliefs are highly inaccurate and create the illusion that we know much more about ourselves than we in fact do.

5.4.3 The Bias Blind Spot

Given its connection with people's overestimation of their cognitive performance relative to others and its direct relevance to the problem of disagreement, I will now take a look at the phenomenon of the *bias blind spot*.[38] Before doing so, let us say what bias is. The term "bias" is typically used to refer either to a cognitive process or to a type of error. As a cognitive process, a bias is an unconscious tendency to make judgments or decisions that are mistaken, unjustified, or suboptimal inasmuch as they do not accord with what are taken to be correct rational standards. As a type of error, a bias is an error that is systematic and that can be of two kinds: an error that is caused by failure to know or apply a rule of inference, or an error that is caused by the influence of a bias understood as a cognitive process (see Wilson & Brekke 1994).

The blind spot in bias perception occurs when one observes an asymmetry in susceptibility to bias between oneself and others: one mistakenly sees oneself as less susceptible to cognitive and motivational biases than others are. Given that the bias blind spot prevents us from recognizing the influence of biases on ourselves, it has been characterized as a "metabias" or "metacognitive bias" (West *et al.* 2012: 507, 513–514; Scopelliti *et al.* 2015: 2470, 2478, 2482–2483). This metabias is explained by three factors: self-enhancement, naïve realism, and the introspection illusion.

Self-enhancement is the tendency to create a positive view of oneself by denying susceptibility to biases that are socially undesirable. Naïve realism is the assumption that our opinions about people, objects, and events in the world are accurate perceptions of an objective reality that are shared by other open-minded and impartial truth seekers who have the same information as we do about those people, objects, and events. As a result, when others do not share our opinions, we tend to explain this disagreement either as reflecting their

---

[38] On this issue, see Pronin *et al.* (2002, 2004), Ehrlinger *et al.* (2005), Frantz (2006), Pronin (2007), Pronin & Kugler (2007), Elashi & Mills (2015), Scopelliti *et al.* (2015), Ross *et al.* (2016), Kukucka *et al.* (2017), and Cheek & Pronin (2022).

ignorance or misinformation, or as resulting from the distorting influence of various biases that prevent them from having accurate perceptions of reality or from drawing reasonable conclusions from the available information.[39]

Most of what we think we know about ourselves is considered to be gained through introspection. However, both psychologists and philosophers have provided ample evidence that we have little or no privileged and reliable introspective access both to the cognitive processes underlying our choices, judgments, inferences, and behavior,[40] and to our current conscious phenomenology.[41] We are thus subject to an introspection illusion, which is our tendency to overvalue introspection as a reliable means of gaining self-insight when in fact introspective information is dramatically limited and highly misleading.[42] This illusion contains three elements:

> (i) it occurs when people are considering their own (as opposed to other people's) introspections; (ii) it involves a trade-off between the consideration of introspective information (e.g. thoughts, feelings, motives) versus other information (e.g. behavioral information, naïve theories, population base rates); and (iii) it results not simply from plentiful access to introspective information (of the sort actors, but not observers, typically have) but from the perceived diagnostic value of that information. (Pronin 2007: 38–39)

When people examine whether their judgments and inferences are biased, they rely heavily on introspective information: they think that, if they were biased, they would be aware of it. However, given that the influence of bias typically occurs unconsciously, the result of their introspective self-assessment is that there is no such influence: they find no phenomenological trace of the bias. By contrast, when they examine whether others have succumbed to bias, they rely on information deriving from external sources, such as observable behavior and general theories of what biased behavior looks like. This asymmetry in the information used to evaluate oneself and others is related to a set of biases known as illusions of asymmetric insight, which result from the conviction that while knowing oneself requires having access to one's private thoughts, feelings, and intentions, knowing others is possible by attending solely to their behaviors, gestures, and verbal responses (Pronin *et al.* 2001, 2004: 794). Under the influence of those illusions, one believes that one knows others better than they know oneself, that one knows oneself better than others know themselves, and that one knows others better than they know themselves.

---

[39] Pronin *et al.* (2002: 369, 378–379), Pronin *et al.* (2004: 781, 783), Pronin (2007: 39–40), Cheek & Pronin (2022: 49). For an in-depth analysis of naïve realism, see especially Ross & Ward (1996).

[40] See, e.g., Nisbett & Wilson (1977), Wilson & Nisbett (1978), and Wilson (2002).

[41] See especially Schwitzgebel (2011).

[42] See Pronin (2007, 2009) and Pronin & Kugler (2007); also Pronin *et al.* (2004: 783–784, 791–792).

The third element of the introspection illusion mentioned in the quoted passage is particularly relevant to the discussion of whether appealing to personal information is an effective strategy for dealing with disagreements. For, by my lights, proponents of that strategy would deny that the dialectical symmetry between disputants who both appeal to personal information has any epistemic implications on the basis that, from one's own first-person perspective, the personal information of one's opponent is not as valuable as one's own personal information. As Pronin points out, although self-other differences in the weighing of introspective information reflect the fact that people have far more access to their own introspections than to others', those differences are also due to the greater value people assign to their own introspections:

> Studies have shown that: (i) people report that internal information is a more valuable source of information about their own bias than others' bias; (ii) people show a bias blind spot even when they have detailed access to others' introspections; and (iii) people believe that an actor's bias is more aptly defined by introspective contents when that actor is themselves rather than someone else. (Pronin 2007: 39)

In evaluating whether others are biased, we rely on abstract theories rather than on introspective reports because we regard these reports with skepticism: we know that people are capable of deceiving both others and themselves (Ehrlinger *et al.* 2005: 681–682, 686). Interestingly, in one study conducted by Pronin and Matthew Kugler (2007: 573), the great majority of observers who had access to actors' introspective reports viewed these reports as faithful accounts of the actors' ongoing thoughts. Nevertheless, they saw the actors as more biased than the latter saw themselves and, moreover, attributed to the actors amounts of bias that were similar to those attributed by observers who did not have access to the introspective reports. The crucial question is whether the asymmetry in the valuation of our own introspections and those of our opponents is legitimate. If the reason for such an asymmetry is simply that the former introspections are our own, then our assignment of greater value to them is arbitrary. If the reason is rather our suspicion that others may be deceiving themselves, then we should remember that we, too, are capable of deceiving ourselves. If knowing about our opponent's introspective information is insufficient to change our perception of bias in him because we take the influence of bias to be typically unconscious, then what is so special about our own introspective information that enables us to legitimately and confidently claim that we are free from such biasing influence?

From what we have seen thus far, there is a close connection between one's perception of bias in others and one's reaction to disagreement. In this regard, some studies have provided evidence that people are particularly blind to their own biases or to those of their allies in situations of disagreement: they are able to recognize biased responses in others who disagree with them, but not in themselves or those who share their opinions. In a series of studies on the liking bias – the tendency to favor the side one likes – while participants "seemed fully aware that liking influences the judgments of others," they "maintained that their natural likes and dislikes did not influence their responses, even though these preferences correlated with their conclusions about the conflict" (Frantz 2006: 160). They thought that, unlike their opponents, they were trying to be fair, to consider the facts, and to see both sides. As Cynthia Frantz (2006: 166) notes, the conflicts used in her studies were ones in which participants were not personally involved, and it is reasonable to assume that the biasing effects of their affective preferences would have been more dramatic if the conflicts had involved people whom participants knew or if they themselves had been parties to those conflicts.[43] It is also worth noting that Frantz takes the bias blind spot to explain the previously documented backfire effect occurring when people are motivated to be fair: in two studies, participants were encouraged to be fair when examining both sides of a conflict so as to help them correct their liking bias (Franz & Janoff-Bulman 2000). However, this fairness motivation back-fired: although participants did put more effort into thinking about the conflict, the effort did not eliminate bias. Moreover, those who had a preference for one side over another focused their extra effort on supporting their own side rather than on rethinking the credentials of the rival side (Franz & Janoff-Bulman 2000). The bias blind spot would explain this result as follows: when people are encouraged to be fair but find no introspective evidence of bias, they state more emphatically their views on the disputed matter. Although they have a naïve theory according to which liking biases both sides of a dispute, they are unable to detect this bias in their own views because it is unavailable to consciousness (Frantz 2006: 158).

Applied to the phenomenon of disagreement and the appeal to personal information as a symmetry breaker, the studies that have been reviewed give rise to the worry that, when relying on one's assessment of that information to support one's own view and to downgrade one's opponent's, one may be a victim

---

[43] The fact that one views those who agree with one as less susceptible to bias is explained by naïve realism: given that one takes one's own beliefs about the world to represent it as it really is, one will not regard those who share one's beliefs as biased unless one has a reason to do so that is independent of their holding those beliefs. On this, see Kelly (2022: 93–94, 98–100), who nonetheless prefers his "perspectival account of bias attributions" to naïve realism. I think that, in the end, there is no difference between the two explanations because – despite the lack of clarity of some psychologists – the key to naïve realism is the tendency to view one's own beliefs as true rather than as unbiased.

of bias without realizing it. The existence of the bias blind spot thus provides a further reason to doubt that self-assessment based on personal information is an effective strategy for resolving disagreements from a first-person perspective. We can apply here the considerations of Section 5.3 concerning the dialectical-cum-epistemic symmetry between the disputants. I remarked that, once each disputant becomes aware that they both appeal to personal information to retain their beliefs and to infer that there is some sort of epistemic failure or deficiency on their opponent's part, each disputant acquires higher-order evidence to the effect that one may be highly confident in one's personal-information-based assessment of one's epistemic situation even though one is mistaken in one's belief. It may similarly be argued that, once each disputant becomes aware that they both believe that they are less susceptible to bias than their opponent, each disputant acquires higher-order evidence to the effect that one may be highly confident, on the basis of introspection, that one is not biased even though one is actually a victim of bias. The person who remains highly confident that her position is correct because of the personal information she possesses, even after being confronted with the fact that her opponent equally appeals to personal information to ground his confidence in the opposite position, is reacting in the same way as the person who remains highly confident that she is not biased because of the introspective information she possesses, even after being confronted with the fact that her opponent equally appeals to introspective information to ground his confidence that he is not biased. In both cases, the higher-order evidence is dismissed out of hand or, at least, is not given proper consideration.[44]

It is worth noting that experimental studies have shown that cognitive sophistication does not attenuate the bias blind spot with respect to the classic cognitive biases studied in the literature on heuristics and biases, and that a larger bias blind spot is actually associated with higher cognitive ability (West *et al.* 2012). Even psychologists succumb to the bias blind spot: in a recent study, forensic psychologists perceived themselves as less vulnerable to bias than their colleagues and believed that introspection is an effective

---

[44] Kelly (2022: 222–229) rejects the kind of skeptical stance I defend here on the grounds that the literature on the bias blind spot does not suggest that (a) people are equally biased in their beliefs about controversial issues or that (b) they are equally reliable in their judgments about who is biased and who is not. In his view, there are relevant asymmetries between the disputants with respect to (a) and (b) mainly because people differ in the accuracy of their first-order judgments. In reply, note, first, that the bias blind spot is only one of the bricks that are used to build the skeptical case. Second, we are in the dark about the above asymmetries inasmuch as we do not seem to have principled ways to identify who is less biased about controversial issues or more reliable in detecting biased people. Third, the skeptic's whole point in calling attention to the thorny epistemic problems raised by disagreement is to show that it is no easy task to determine – from both a third- and a first-person perspective – whose first-order judgments are accurate.

strategy for detecting the influence of bias in their own judgments (Neal & Brodsky 2016). Thus, it seems that we cannot even trust experts or members of the cognitive elites to recognize, when they are engaged in a disagreement, that they may well have fallen prey to bias without having any introspective evidence of it, and that they cannot simply dismiss their peers' opposing judgments on the grounds that they are biased.

5.4.4 Confirmation Bias

Psychological findings indicate that, with regard to controversial matters, disputants tend to seek, generate, evaluate, assimilate, or recall evidence in a biased manner. In a classic paper, Charles Lord, Lee Ross, and Mark Lepper (1979) exposed the parties to the dispute about the deterrent efficacy of capital punishment to the same mixed and inconclusive empirical evidence. They found that subjects accepted at face value evidence that confirmed their views but critically evaluated disconfirming evidence – a phenomenon that they call "biased assimilation" and that has come to be known as "motivated reasoning," "confirmation bias," or "myside bias."[45] In addition, instead of leading to moderation and narrowing the disagreement, exposure to mixed and inconclusive evidence led the pro- and anti-capital punishment groups to increased polarization. Thus, because of their biased assessment of the evidence, all the parties to a dispute can have their views strengthened by the very same body of evidence. These results have been replicated in dozens of studies that focus on other controversial issues, such as homosexuality and gun control (Munro & Ditto 1997; Kahan *et al.* 2017).

One reason the studies under consideration are important is that the kind of controversies on which they focus are not idealized but real-life disagreements, disagreements over issues that are emotionally charged and regarding which the available evidence is often mixed and far from conclusive. Another reason for their significance is that those studies show that all the parties to a dispute may exhibit the bias of seeking, generating, evaluating, assimilating, or recalling evidence in a manner that is partial to their preexisting beliefs, hypotheses, or expectations. When that happens, how can one impartially decide which of the disputants, if any, is right about the contested matter? It might be argued that if one's prior beliefs, hypotheses, or expectations are on the right track, then it is not irrational for one's evidence processing to be partial to them (cf. Stanovich 2021: chap. 2). The problem is that one's opponent can use the same line of

---

[45] Although the concepts in question (especially motivated reasoning and confirmation bias) are sometimes distinguished, they are frequently used to refer to the same range of flawed information processing tendencies. On this (family of) bias(es), see also Mahoney (1977), Kunda (1990), Ditto & Lopez (1992), Munro & Ditto (1997), Nickerson (1998), Lord & Taylor (2009), Hahn & Harris (2014), Kahan *et al.* (2017), Mercier (2017), and Stanovich (2021).

argument, and the disagreement consists precisely in the fact that each party regards the other's view on the contested matter as being on the wrong track. The whole point of full disclosure is to have both parties examine, as much as possible, the very same body of evidence so as to determine who has made a mistake in evaluating it. Confirmation bias and the resulting belief polarization represent a formidable obstacle to the attainment of that goal.

Cognitive psychologist Keith Stanovich's latest book is devoted to confirmation bias, which he prefers to call "myside bias" (2021: 5 with n. 2). He remarks that this bias is an "outlier bias" because, unlike most biases, it cannot be predicted from standard measures of cognitive abilities – such as intelligence and numeracy – and thinking dispositions – such as open-mindedness and need for cognition (2021: chap. 3). This explains why myside bias creates a blind spot among cognitive elites, who take themselves to be less biased than other people (2021: chap. 5). Although they are often right because "cognitive sophistication is moderately correlated with the ability to avoid . . . most biases," myside bias is "the bias where the cognitive elites most often think they are unbiased when in fact they are just as biased as everyone else" (2021: xi). As Stanovich remarks, not only does myside bias occur "in a wide variety of judgment domains" and not only may it occur "in every stage of information processing," but it "is displayed by people in all demographic groups, and it is exhibited even by expert reasoners, the highly educated, and the highly intelligent" (2021: 1). Among these are the social scientists studying myside bias who typically have a strong commitment to an ideological viewpoint – virtually all are liberal progressists. They mistakenly believe that their high cognitive abilities, high education, and positive thinking dispositions render them immune to that bias, when in fact they are subject to myside bias just as much as their conservative opponents (2021: 96–100). Moreover, some studies have provided evidence that individuals with higher levels of scientific reasoning skills, education, knowledge, or numeracy show greater myside bias (2021: 58–61). Thus, greater cognitive sophistication not only does not render us immune from myside bias but might even increase it. As we saw in Section 5.4.3, something similar occurs with respect to the bias blind spot.

For present purposes, the importance of the distinctiveness of myside bias lies in that, even though from a first-person perspective one might come to the conclusion that one's own view on the disputed matter is to be preferred to that of one's opponent because one has reliable information about one's education, training, cognitive abilities, and thinking dispositions, one's view might nonetheless be epistemically distorted. Knowing about the blind spot created by myside bias provides us with another strong reason to doubt that the personal-information strategy is effective.

Note also that cognitive psychology does not tell us that the members of the cognitive elites are one hundred percent shielded from the influence of biases other than myside bias.[46] Now, they often disagree among themselves and are regarded as roughly epistemic peers as far as their education, training, cognitive abilities, thinking dispositions, and familiarity with the relevant evidence are concerned. In certain cases, they explain the disagreement of their peers by appealing to the distorting influence of bias (a striking example is Fumerton 2010: 102–105). From a first-person perspective, I can ask myself: if my rival has fallen prey to one or more biases despite having an education, a training, cognitive abilities, thinking dispositions, and evidence that are roughly similar to mine, how can I rule out the possibility that I (too) have fallen victim to one or more biases? Note, finally, that the fact that members of the cognitive elites often disagree among themselves and the fact that they may well be under the distorting influence of bias shows that appealing to them to resolve disputes presents one with further challenges: one needs to determine which member of a cognitive elite one should follow, whether their disagreements are to be explained by some or all of them having fallen victim to bias, and if so, to which bias.[47]

5.4.5 Noise

Bias and noise are considered to be two types of error in human judgment. While bias is systematic and hence can be predicted, noise is random and hence unpredictable. For example, if a team of shooters is biased, they are systematic-ally off target and one can predict the next shot by looking at the previous ones; but if the team is noisy, the prediction is impossible because the previous shots are widely scattered. The shooters, though, can be both biased and noisy: their shots can be systematically off target while at the same time being widely scattered (Kahneman *et al.* 2021: 3–4).

Applied to human judgment, noise is variability or disagreement: doctors making different judgments about what disease is affecting a patient, case

---

[46] Experimental research has provided evidence that various epistemically irrelevant factors heavily influence philosophers' judgments despite their extensive training, reasoning skills, and alleged expertise (see Schulz *et al.* 2011; Schwitzgebel & Cushman 2012, 2015; Tobia *et al.* 2013; Tobia *et al.* 2013; Vaesen *et al.* 2013).

[47] A reviewer has remarked that, in their interpretation of the data, the psychologists who study confirmation bias and other epistemically contaminating factors either (i) have been able to avoid their influence and, if so, why can we not all avoid it? or (ii) have not avoided it and, if so, can we trust the results of their studies? Granting that people in general are vulnerable to epistemically contaminating factors, I think that the extreme difficulty in determining precisely who is under their influence, when, and to what extent only boosts the skeptical vertigo induced by awareness of the epistemic challenge posed by disagreement.

managers in child protection services making different decisions on whether a child is at risk of abuse, professional forecasters making highly variable predictions about the likely sales of a product or the likelihood of bankruptcy of a company, judges making radically different decisions on whether to admit an asylum seeker into a country or on whether an accused person will be granted bail or sent to jail pending trial (Kahneman *et al.* 2021: 6–7).

What interests me is occasion noise, which is "the variability in judgments of the same case by the same person or group on different occasions" (Kahneman *et al.* 2021: 8). One form of occasion noise is then within-person variability or, as I prefer to call it, intrapersonal disagreement, of which we can give the following examples. Judges are more likely to grant parole at the beginning of the day or after a food break than immediately before the break (Danziger *et al.* 2011); they make harsher decisions after their football team lost a game (Eren & Mocan 2018; Chen & Loecher 2022); they are more indulgent with the defendant if it is the latter's birthday (Chen & Philippe 2023); they are less likely to grant asylum if it is hot outside (Heyes & Saberian 2019). At the end of a long day, doctors are more likely to prescribe opioids (Philpot *et al.* 2018; Neprash & Barnett 2019) or antibiotics (Linder *et al.* 2014) and less likely to order cancer screenings (Hsiang *et al.* 2019). After a series of decisions that go in the same direction, judges, loan officers, and baseball empires are more likely to make a decision in the opposite direction to restore balance (Chen *et al.* 2016). Granted, these studies do not refer to different judgments and decisions about the very same case made by the very same person. However, first, many of the cases regarding which diverging judgments and decisions were made were relevantly similar. Second, one may reasonably infer that the same person would have made a different judgment and decision about the same case if the irrelevant factor that has affected his actual judgment and decision had been different. The same considerations apply to the studies, referred to in Section 5.4.2, that have explored the influence of epistemically irrelevant factors on moral judgments and voting decisions.

Kahneman, Sibony, and Sunstein themselves remark that, even though noise is unwanted variability in judgments that should ideally be identical, there may be noise in singular decisions on account of the same factors that cause noise in recurrent decisions. Consider the following passage:

> If we observed only the first shooter on the [noisy] team, we would have no idea how noisy the team is, but the sources of noise would still be there. Similarly, when you make a singular decision, you have to imagine that another decision maker, even one just as competent as you and sharing the same goals and values, would not reach the same conclusion from the same facts. And as the decision maker, you should recognize that you might have

made a different decision if some irrelevant aspects of the situation or of the decision-making process had been different.

In other words, we cannot measure noise in a singular decision, but if we think counterfactually, we know for sure that noise is there. Just as the shooter's unsteady hand implies that a single shot *could* have landed somewhere else, noise in the decision makers and in the decision-making process implies that the singular decision *could* have been different. (2021: 37)

The authors are here referring to counterfactual interpersonal and intrapersonal disagreements. Let us focus on the latter: one judges that *p* but, if the circumstances had been different, one would have judged that not-*p* or suspended judgment about whether *p*. Suppose that I am a Catholic because I was born in France, where Catholicism is the main religion, but I would have been a Buddhist had I been born in China, where Buddhism is the main religion. Place of birth seems to be an epistemically irrelevant factor, and so it seems that the disagreement between my actual self and my counterfactual self is unresolvable unless I have a compelling reason to believe that my religious beliefs are in fact right, and so that I was lucky enough to have been born in France. Another typical example of this kind of counterfactual intrapersonal disagreement concerns the university one attended: suppose that I believe in free will because I studied philosophy at Oxford University, but that I would have believed in determinism had I studied philosophy at the University of Geneva. Again, it might be argued that the disagreement is unresolvable unless I have a compelling reason to believe that the theory of free will is in fact true, and so that I was lucky enough to have studied at Oxford. Now, I might nonetheless believe that I am smart, insightful, and unbiased enough that I would still have been a Catholic had I been born in China (provided I had been exposed to Catholicism), and that I would still have believed in free will had I attended the University of Geneva. Thus, my counterfactual self would not disagree with my actual self. Similarly, a judge who has imposed a severe sentence after his football team lost a game or who did not grant asylum on a hot day might argue that he would have made the same judgments and corresponding decisions had the circumstances been different, and that in similar cases his judgments and decisions were different due to certain relevant specific features of those cases.

Fortunately for my line of argument, we do not need to content ourselves with merely *counterfactual* intrapersonal disagreements. For other studies show that there are *actual* intrapersonal disagreements. Here are some examples: the same experienced software developers gave, on two separate days, radically different estimates for the completion time for the same task (Grimstad & Jørgensen 2007); the same forensic examiners sometimes reached different conclusions when presented twice with the same fingerprint (Dror & Charlton 2006; Dror *et al.* 2006; Dror & Rosenthal 2008; Dror *et al.* 2011; Ulery *et al.* 2012); the same physicians often made different judgments when assessing the degree of blockage in the same angiograms (Detre *et al.* 1975); the same radiologists sometimes made different judgments when assessing the same image again (Robinson *et al.* 1999); the same wine experts who, at a major wine competition, tasted the same wines twice gave the same score to only 18 percent of the wines (Hodgson 2008).[48]

These studies should block the overconfident or hubristic beliefs of those who deny that they would disagree with their counterfactual selves. For they show that there is actual occasion noise: people do form different judgments about the same case depending on the circumstances. We are usually unaware not only of such intrapersonal disagreements, but also of the influence of the epistemically irrelevant factors that are the cause of the occasion noise. So, just as interpersonal disagreement, intrapersonal disagreement is epistemically relevant because it can make us aware of the influence of factors that contaminate our judgments and of the limits of our self-knowledge. Acquiring the higher-order evidence that, sometimes at least, we disagree with ourselves because our judgments are influenced by epistemically distorting factors provides a *prima facie* defeater for the beliefs based on those judgments. We should then withhold those beliefs unless we can justifiably establish that we have not fallen prey to such a contaminating influence or unless we can come up with effective ways to neutralize it.

A point worth emphasizing is that the actual occasion noise detected in the above studies concerns carefully considered judgments made by experts, which invites three considerations. First, even those who are supposed to be highly qualified in a given domain may, unbeknownst to them, disagree with themselves about a given issue in that domain under the influence of epistemically distorting factors. This shows both that experts are not immune from being contaminated by those factors and that their self-knowledge is, in this respect, disturbingly limited. Second, which of the conflicting judgments made by the same expert should one trust or rely on when trying to make up one's mind about a disputed issue? Third, even if one does not observe that an expert whom one is consulting disagrees with himself, one may well ask – after reading the above studies – whether the expert would not disagree with himself if certain epistemically irrelevant factors were different.

Kahneman, Sibony, and Sunstein remark time and again that people are typically entirely oblivious to noise (2021: 9, 32, 220, 257, 324, 375).

---

[48] In none of these cases, of course, were the persons making the conflicting judgments aware that they were presented with the same evidence.

It seems that system noise[49] is in principle more easily identifiable given that one can *observe*, from the outside, people disagreeing with each other.[50] By contrast, it is no surprise that at least the great majority of us are unaware that we disagree with ourselves depending on the day of the week, our current mood, the outside temperature, or our feeling of hunger. For we do not pay attention to those circumstances or conditions, and to their change over time, as being epistemically relevant.

As noted in Section 1, intrapersonal disagreement is relevant to interpersonal disagreement when one tends to be overconfident or hubristic when others reject one's views. For if one's disagreements with oneself are at least sometimes to be explained by the influence of epistemically distorting factors that cloud one's judgments, then one can legitimately assume that one's disagreements with others are at least sometimes to be explained by one's falling prey to the same factors. For why would one be immune to their influence in the latter case but not in the former? Note also that, just as with interpersonal disagreement, when one disagrees with oneself, one is confronted with the difficulty of determining whether or when one's judgments are contaminated by epistemically irrelevant factors. For example, it may be difficult to determine whether, when one abandons a previous judgment and forms a contrary one, the change is to be explained by (i) the fact that, although one objectively and accurately assessed the evidence when forming both judgments, more relevant evidence became available when forming the new one; or (ii) the fact that, while one's former judgment was formed under the influence of epistemically distorting factors, one's new judgment is the result of an objective and accurate assessment of the evidence; or (iii) the fact that, while one's former judgment was properly formed, the formation of the new judgment was contaminated by epistemically irrelevant factors; or (iv) the fact that both judgments are contaminated by such factors.

The results of the experimental studies that have been reviewed in Section 5.4 show that it is unrealistic to view the possession of personal information and the ineliminability of the first-person perspective as symmetry breakers in most disagreements. For the available personal information is often radically misleading and the first-person perspective does not prevent us from realizing how

---

[49] System noise is the undesirable variability in the judgments or decisions regarding the same case by multiple interchangeable individuals (Kahneman *et al.* 2021: 78, 363).

[50] Note, however, that just as one usually needs to conduct a study in which the same person is asked to assess the same case on different occasions in order to detect occasion noise, so too sometimes does one need to conduct an audit in an organization consisting in asking many individuals to evaluate the same case, or very similar cases, in order to make visible the variability in their responses. Without such an audit, there is an "illusion of agreement" (Kahneman *et al.* 2021: 30). This illusion of agreement is in part explained by naïve realism inasmuch as, unless disagreement is revealed, we think that others see the world as we do (2021: 31).

limited our self-knowledge is. Becoming aware of the wide-ranging influence of epistemically distorting factors on our judgments and decisions should render us much more cautious in holding beliefs about controversial matters. Note also that those experimental studies represent a threat not only to epistemic internalism but also to epistemic externalism. For the epistemic challenge they pose is not only that we do not have reflective access to our belief-forming processes and cannot tell whether or when we are under the influence of epistemically distorting factors, but also that those belief-forming processes are often unreliable.[51]

5.5 Unpossessed Information about Others

When epistemic peerhood is understood as consisting in perfect cognitive and evidential parity between the disputants, the conclusions arrived at in the debate on the epistemic significance of peer disagreement cannot be fully carried over to real-world disputes.[52] For it is hard to believe that two flesh-and-blood individuals are both equally familiar with the same relevant evidence – particularly when the body of evidence is vast and complex – and that they both possess the very same cognitive abilities. But even if we concede that there are epistemic peers of that kind, it seems very hard to determine that any two individuals are epistemic peers so that one can legitimately talk about a peer disagreement that is acknowledged to be so by the disputants.

It seems more likely that, even though two individuals differ in their access to the relevant evidence and/or in their cognitive abilities, they are both, on the whole, equally good at evaluating the matter under consideration: one disputant's superiority in one aspect (e.g., thoroughness or open-mindedness) may compensate for his inferiority in another (e.g., intelligence or limited background knowledge). Note, however, that even if we grant that there exist epistemic peers in this less stringent sense, it still seems quite difficult to determine, in real-life situations, that any two individuals are epistemic equals in that sense because one would have to possess a great deal of accurate information about their epistemic positions.

Given the actual conditions of real-life disputes, which are far from perfectly transparent, it may seem that suspension is the attitude to be adopted in those very few cases in which there is some sort of epistemic peerhood. However,

---

[51] If people have good reason to conciliate in the light of their discovery of significant disagreement even if they are completely ignorant of the empirical studies reviewed in Section 5.4, are those studies merely icing on the cake? I think they provide an additional key reason to conciliate as they show that adopting the first-person perspective or relying on personal information can hardly function as symmetry breakers.

[52] Cf. Frances (2010: 424–425, 2014: 45–46), Lackey (2010: 303–305), King (2012: 251–266, 2013: 199–201), and Sherman (2015: 426–428).

even if we set acknowledged peer disagreement aside and focus instead on real-world disputes with all their complexities, skepticism is not out of the picture, but actually becomes more threatening. Notice that even if it were granted for the sake of argument that accurate self-assessment is possible because we have extensive self-knowledge, one often has no or partial information about one's opponent's evidence, the reliability (or lack thereof) of his cognitive abilities, or the functioning of these abilities in the specific circumstance of the disagreement. Such total or partial lack of information poses a serious challenge because it means that we are in the dark about information that must be taken into consideration when deciding what to believe about the disputed matter, and hence that it is no easy task to determine which, if any, of the disputants is in a better epistemic position with regard to that matter (cf. King 2012: 251, 267). One's total or partial ignorance of one's opponent's epistemic situation should make one wonder whether he may not possess relevant evidence that one lacks, whether he may not have higher cognitive abilities, or whether he may not be employing his cognitive abilities to assess the disputed matter better than one is employing one's own. None of these possibilities can be easily excluded in at least many cases of real-life disagreement. If so, then one should refrain from believing that, when engaged in a disagreement, one can often legitimately downgrade one's opponent on the basis of one's personal information despite one's total or partial ignorance of his epistemic standing. Otherwise, one would be making a judgment on the basis of limited relevant information. In the face of real-life disagreements, one had better remind oneself of paying attention to both available and unpossessed information (cf. Ballantyne 2019: chap. 7). To appreciate this, try to remember those occasions in which you downgraded an opponent because of your high degree of confidence in how smart, informed, meticulous, and objective you were in your analysis of the disputed matter, just to later realize that you were mistaken and that you should have been more open-minded and intellectually humble: your opponent turned out to be smarter or better informed or more meticulous or less biased.

With regard to one's lack of (full) access to one's dissenter's (total) evidence, the case of religious experience – a topic touched on in Section 4 – is particularly relevant. Consider the claim made by many religious believers to the effect that they have had visions and auditions (through their eyes and ears or in a nonphysical way), or ineffable mystical insights, or a direct awareness of the presence of God. Suppose that you are engaged in a disagreement about the epistemic justification of religious belief with someone who makes such a claim. How should you react? Should you explain it away on naturalistic grounds, arguing that he is merely delusional? Or should you rather entertain the possibility that your dissenter has had a veridical experience of a kind that is (so far at least) entirely foreign to you? It is possible that he is lying and that you have no hint that he is doing so, in which case you would still lack crucial information, namely, information to the effect that his report should be dismissed out of hand. But, as noted in Section 4, one need not question that people in general have religious experiences; the key issue concerns the veridicality of such experiences. If you have never had such an experience (as in my case), then you lack a kind of experience that may be key in determining the justification of religious belief inasmuch as there might be relevant information that can only be obtained by having that experience – full disclosure does not seem feasible in at least most instances of religious experience (cf. Pittard 2019: 183). Or if you have had an experience of that kind but have dismissed it as non-veridical, perhaps your dissenter's specific religious experience is different from your own in a crucial way or perhaps your dissenter is open enough to appreciate the full epistemic significance of religious experience. Imagine that it is Alson or Plantinga or some other Christian philosopher whose positive epistemic credentials you recognize who claims to have had a religious experience he takes to be veridical. One can assume that philosophers of such caliber have carefully considered the possibility that they may be delusional and have come to the conclusion that they are not. Of course, they may well be wrong because they may have fallen prey to certain cognitive or motivational biases despite their general competence and best efforts. The problem is that it is hard to determine whether or not that is the case. Hence, can you rule out the possibility that they have relevant evidence that you lack?

With respect to one's lack of (full) knowledge of one's dissenter's (full range of) cognitive capacities and their reliability, another religious example may be illuminating. How should you react if your rival in the disagreement about the epistemic justification of religious belief claims that he forms his theistic beliefs by means of a special cognitive faculty – such as the *sensus divinitatis* – that God have implanted in us? Should you affirm that he is merely delusional in believing that such a capacity exists, that he possesses it, and that it is reliable? Or should you rather entertain the possibility that he may have a different cognitive capacity by means of which he comes to a different view on the subject of the disagreement, or that you both have the same capacity but that yours malfunctions? As far as I am concerned, I feel the pressure to take that possibility seriously, and hence to suspend judgment, when it is Plantinga (2000) and other seemingly competent philosophers who defend the existence of such a cognitive capacity as the *sensus divinitatis*.

In sum, even though I myself am not a religious person, and so even though Alston's (1991) view of the experiential awareness of God and Plantinga's (2000) view of the *sensus divinitatis* are entirely foreign to me, the fact that competent philosophers defend the rationality of religious belief puts pressure on me not to rule out the possibility that they have access to relevant evidence that I do not have, or that they possess a religious belief-producing capacity that I lack, or that we all have such a capacity but that in some of us it malfunctions. This is not to say that very smart people (and people much smarter than I) whose views I do not share are shielded from cognitive and motivational biases and other epistemically contaminating factors. (As we saw in Section 5.4, that is not at all the case.) Rather, it is to recognize that the range of my experiences may be significantly limited and that others may have cognitive abilities that I lack. It is also to recognize that I myself am not shielded from various epistemically contaminating factors either. Given that, at present at least, I have no access to information that is relevant to establishing what the epistemic position of believers is with regard to religious matters, I cannot rule out the possibility that their epistemic position is superior to mine. Maybe people who claim to have certain religious experiences are lying, maybe they do have the experiences they report but are delusional, or maybe their experiences are veridical. In many real-life cases at least, it is extremely hard to determine which is the case.

In sum, we are at least quite often in the dark about relevant information concerning the epistemic position of our dissenters. And if we accept – as argued in Section 5.4 – that people know much less about their evidence, cognitive capacities, and performance than they believe, then there is even more information about which we are in the dark. It is therefore extremely difficult to establish with the required precision what my epistemic situation is in relation to that of my rival – and it is equally difficult for him to do so. If I cannot justifiably affirm that I am epistemically superior to my opponent with regard to the disputed matter, and *vice versa*, then it appears that for both of us suspension is called for. If so, then it is not the case that a broad skepticism threatens only if one restricts oneself to acknowledged peer disagreements. What we do not know both about ourselves and about others poses a serious challenge to the epistemic credentials of our beliefs about controversial matters.[53]

5.6 Skeptical Dogmatism

In present-day epistemology, when awareness of disagreement is taken to lead to a skeptical stance, the skepticism in question is typically agnostic. A different form of disagreement-based skepticism has recently been proposed by Mark Walker (2023), who defends a view he calls "skeptical dogmatism." The skeptical dogmatist maintains that, when confronted with many multi-proposition

---

[53] But not only about controversial matters inasmuch as our beliefs may be, unbeknownst to us, contaminated by epistemically irrelevant factors even when they are not contested by others.

philosophical disagreements (i.e., philosophical disagreements where there are more than two contrary views), the correct doxastic attitude to adopt for the disputants is disbelief (or a degree of confidence below 0.5) rather than suspension inasmuch as all the conflicting views are probably false. For example, if there is a philosophical disagreement between four views that are mutually exclusive, jointly exhaustive, and equally credible, then there is only a 0.25 chance that any one of them is true. Skeptical dogmatism is also to be adopted in the case of a multi-proposition philosophical disagreement in which one or more views are deemed to be more credible than the others but not to the point of being more likely true than not. Thus, in philosophical disagreements such as the two just described, each of the parties should believe that their preferred philosophical view is probably false.

It might be argued that suspension is still called for in the cases considered by Walker. If asked which of the mutually exclusive and jointly exhaustive philosophical views on p is the correct one, the skeptical dogmatist will reply that he does not know or that he cannot decide. Even if, with regard to each individual view, the skeptical dogmatist feels rationally compelled to claim that it is probably false, with regard to the whole set of competing views, he is undecided about which one is correct. Suspension about whether p can be conceived of as a state of indecision reached after having evaluated the competing views on whether p.

6 Conclusion

Disagreement is a ubiquitous phenomenon of our social and inner lives. Its epistemic relevance is severalfold. First, disagreement triggers a demand for justification that cannot be easily met because the competing views may be equally persuasive or because, in the attempt to justify their views, the disputants fall prey to Agrippa's trilemma. This may be taken either as an indication that our beliefs about controversial matters are at least so far unjustified, or as an indication that the truth about such matters cannot be known. Second, the existence of deep, widespread, and persistent disagreements in such areas as morality and religion is a phenomenon that demands an explanation. If the best available explanation is an antirealist one, then our beliefs in those areas are false and first-order knowledge is thereby undermined. If the realist and the antirealist explanations are taken to be on a par, then suspending our beliefs is called for. Third, disagreement may reveal one's evidential limitations by making one realize that others may have different publicly available evidence or different personal experiences. Fourth, disagreement may reveal one's cognitive limitations by making one aware that others may have higher cognitive abilities or even different cognitive abilities. Fifth, disagreement with others or with oneself may reveal one's cognitive deficiencies caused by the widespread and unconscious influence of epistemically contaminating factors. Sixth, reflection on the intractable difficulties encountered in the attempt to resolve real-life disputes – including how much we do not know about our own epistemic standing and our opponents' – may encourage open-mindedness, caution, and intellectual humility, which seem to be cognitive virtues inasmuch as they appear to contribute to the attainment of truth and the avoidance of error.

References

Alston, W. 1988. "Religious Diversity and Perceptual Knowledge of God," *Faith and Philosophy* 5(4): 433–448.

Alston, W. 1991. *Perceiving God*. Cornell University Press.

Ballantyne, N. 2019. *Knowing Our Limits*. Oxford University Press.

Ballantyne, N. & Coffman, E. 2011. "Uniqueness, Evidence, and Rationality," *Philosophers' Imprint* 11(18): 1–6.

Ballantyne, N. & Coffman, E. 2012. "Conciliationism and Uniqueness," *Australasian Journal of Philosophy* 90(4): 657–670.

Ballew, C. & Todorov, A. 2007. "Predicting Political Elections from Rapid and Unreflective Face Judgments," *Proceedings of the National Academy of Sciences* 104(46): 17948–17953.

Barnes, J. 1990. *The Toils of Scepticism*. Cambridge University Press.

Bell, P. & Volckmann, D. 2011. "Knowledge Surveys in General Chemistry: Confidence, Overconfidence, and Performance," *Journal of Chemical Education* 88(11): 1469–1476.

Berger, J., Meredith, M., & Wheeler, S. 2008. "Contextual Priming: Where People Vote Affects How They Vote," *Proceedings of the National Academy of Sciences* 105(26): 8846–8849.

Bergmann, M. 2006. *Justification without Awareness*. Oxford University Press.

Cheek, N. & Pronin, E. 2022. "I'm Right, You're Biased: How We Understand Ourselves and Others." In N. Ballantyne & D. Dunning (eds.), *Reason, Bias, and Inquiry*, 35–59. Oxford University Press.

Chen, D. & Loecher, M. 2022. "Mood and the Malleability of Moral Reasoning: The Impact of Irrelevant Factors on Judicial Decisions," *SSRN Electronic Journal*, September 21: 1–70.

Chen, D., Moskowitz, T., & Shue, K. 2016. "Decision Making under the Gambler's Fallacy: Evidence from Asylum Judges, Loan Officers, and Baseball Umpires," *Quarterly Journal of Economics* 131(3): 1181–1242.

Chen, D. & Philippe, A. 2023. "Clash of Norms: Judicial Leniency on Defendant Birthdays," *Journal of Economic Behavior & Organization* 211: 324–344.

Christensen, D. 2007. "Epistemology of Disagreement: The Good News," *The Philosophical Review* 116(2): 187–217.

Christensen, D. 2009. "Disagreement as Evidence: The Epistemology of Controversy," *Philosophy Compass* 4: 756–767.

Christensen, D. 2011. "Disagreement, Question-Begging and Epistemic Self-Criticism," *Philosophers' Imprint* 11(6): 1–22.

Christensen, D. 2013. "Epistemic Modesty Defended." In Christensen & Lackey 2013, 77–97.

Christensen, D. 2014. "Disagreement and Public Controversy." In J. Lackey (ed.), *Essays in Collective Epistemology*, 142–163. Oxford University Press.

Christensen, D. 2019. "Formulating Independence." In M. Skipper & A. Steglich-Petersen (eds.), *Higher-Order Evidence*, 13–34. Oxford University Press.

Christensen, D. & Lackey, J. (eds.). 2013. *The Epistemology of Disagreement*. Oxford University Press.

Conee, E. 2010. "Rational Disagreement Defended." In Feldman & Warfield 2010, 69–90.

Danziger, S., Levav, J., & Avnaim-Pesso, L. 2011. "Extraneous Factors in Judicial Decisions," *Proceedings of the National Academy of Sciences of the United States of America* 108(17): 6889–6892.

Detre, K., Wright, E., Marvin, M., Murphy, L., & Takaro, T. 1975. "Observer Agreement in Evaluating Coronary Angiograms," *Circulation* 52: 979–986.

Ditto, P. & Lopez, D. 1992. "Motivated Skepticism: Use of Differential Decision Criteria for Preferred and Nonpreferred Conclusions," *Journal of Personality and Social Psychology* 63(4): 568–584.

Douven, I. 2009. "Uniqueness Revisited," *American Philosophical Quarterly* 46(4): 347–361.

Dror, I., Champod, C., Langenburg, G. *et al.* 2011. "Cognitive Issues in Fingerprint Analysis: Inter- and Intra-Expert Consistency and the Effect of a 'Target' Comparison," *Forensic Science International* 208(1–3): 10–17.

Dror, I. & Charlton, D. 2006. "Why Experts Make Errors," *Journal of Forensic Identification* 56(4): 600–616.

Dror, I., Charlton, D., & Péron, A. 2006. "Contextual Information Renders Experts Vulnerable to Making Erroneous Identifications," *Forensic Science International* 156(1): 74–78.

Dror, I. & Rosenthal, R. 2008. "Meta-analytically Quantifying the Reliability and Biasability of Forensic Experts," *Journal of Forensic Science* 53(4): 900–903.

Edwards, R., Kellner, K., Sistron, C. & Magyari, E. 2003. "Medical Student Self-Assessment of Performance on an Obstetrics and Gynecology Clerkship," *American Journal of Obstetrics and Gynecology* 188(4): 1078–1082.

Ehrlinger, J., Gilovich, T., & Ross, L. 2005. "Peering into the Bias Spot: People's Assessments of Bias in Themselves and Others," *Personality and Social Psychology Bulletin* 31(5): 680–692.

Ehrlinger, J., Johnson, K., Banner, M., Dunning, D., & Kruger, J. 2008. "Why the Unskilled Are Unaware: Further Explorations of (Absent) Self-Insight among the Incompetent," *Organizational Behavior and Human Decision Processes* 105: 98–121.

Elashi, F. & Mills, C. 2015. "Developing the Bias Blind Spot: Increasing Skepticism towards Others," *PLoS ONE* 10(11): e0141809.

Elga, A. 2007. "Reflection and Disagreement," *Noûs* 41(3): 478–502.

Elga, A. 2010. "How to Disagree about How to Disagree." In Feldman & Warfield 2010, 175–186.

Enoch, D. 2010. "Not Just a Truthometer: Taking Oneself Seriously (but Not Too Seriously) in Cases of Peer Disagreement," *Mind* 119(476): 953–997.

Eren, O. & Mocan, N. 2018. "Emotional Judges and Unlucky Juveniles," *American Economic Journal: Applied Economics* 10(3): 171–205.

Eskine, K., Kacinik, N., & Prinz, J. 2011. "A Bad Taste in the Mouth: Gustatory Disgust Influences Moral Judgment," *Psychological Science* 22(3): 295–299.

Feldman, R. 2003. "Plantinga on Exclusivism," *Faith and Philosophy* 20(1): 85–90.

Feldman, R. 2006. "Epistemological Puzzles about Disagreement." In S. Hetherington (ed.), *Epistemology Futures*, 216–236. Oxford University Press.

Feldman, R. 2007. "Reasonable Religious Disagreements." In L. Antony (ed.), *Philosophers without Gods*, 194–214. Oxford University Press.

Feldman, R. 2021. "Is There Something Special about Religious Disagreement?" In M. Benton & J. Kvanvig (eds.), *Religious Disagreement & Pluralism*, 108–126. Oxford University Press.

Feldman, R. & Warfield, T. (eds.). 2010. *Disagreement*. Oxford University Press.

Foley, R. 2001. *Intellectual Trust in Oneself and Others*. Cambridge University Press.

Frances, B. 2010. "The Reflective Epistemic Renegade," *Philosophy and Phenomenological Research* 81(2): 419–463.

Frances, B. 2014. *Disagreement*. Polity Press.

Frantz, C. 2006. "I Am Being Fair: The Bias Blind Spot as a Stumbling Block to Seeing Both Sides," *Basic and Applied Social Psychology* 28(2): 157–167.

Frantz, C. & Janoff-Bulman, R. 2000. "Considering Both Sides: The Limits of Perspective Taking," *Basic and Applied Social Psychology* 22(1): 31–42.

French, L., Garry, M., & Loftus, E. 2009. "False Memories: A Kind of Confabulation in Non-clinical Patients." In W. Hirstein (ed.), *Confabulation*, 33–66. Oxford University Press.

Fumerton, R. 2010. "You Can't Trust a Philosopher." In Feldman & Warfield 2010, 91–110.

Goldman, A. 1986. *Epistemology and Cognition*. Harvard University Press.

Grimstad, S. & Jørgensen, M. 2007. "Inconsistency of Expert Judgment-Based Estimates of Software Development Effort," *Journal of Systems and Software* 80(11): 1770–1777.

Gutting, G. 1982. *Religious Belief and Religious Skepticism*. University of Notre Dame Press.

Hahn, U. & Harris, A. 2014. "What Does It Mean to Be Biased: Motivated Reasoning and Rationality." In B. Ross (ed.), *Psychology of Learning and Motivation*, volume 61, 41–102. Elsevier.

Haidt, J. 2001. "The Emotional Dog and Its Rational Tail: A Social Intuitionist Approach to Moral Judgment," *Psychological Review* 108(4): 814–834.

Haidt, J. 2013. *The Righteous Mind*. Vintage Books.

Haun, D., Zeringue, A., Leach, A., & Foley, A. 2000. "Assessing the Competence of Specimen-Processing Personnel," *Laboratory Medicine* 31: 633–637.

Heyes, A. & Saberian, S. 2019. "Temperature and Decisions: Evidence from 207,000 Court Cases," *American Economic Journal: Applied Economics* 11(2): 238–265.

Hick, J. 1988. "Religious Pluralism and Salvation," *Faith and Philosophy* 5(4): 365–377.

Hick, J. 1997. "The Epistemological Challenge of Religious Pluralism," *Faith and Philosophy* 14(3): 277–286.

Hick, J. 2004. *An Interpretation of Religion*. Yale University Press.

Hirstein, W. 2005. *Brain Fiction*. The MIT Press.

Hodges, B., Regehr, G., & Martin, D. 2001. "Difficulties in Recognizing One's Own Incompetence: Novice Physicians Who Are Unskilled and Unaware of It," *Academic Medicine* 76: S87–S89.

Hodgson, R. 2008. "An Examination of Judge Reliability at a Major U.S. Wine Competition," *Journal of Wine Economics* 3(2): 105–113.

Horberg, E., Oveis, C., Keltner, D., & Cohen, A. 2009. "Disgust and the Moralization of Purity," *Journal of Personality and Social Psychology* 97(6): 963–976.

Hsiang, E., Mehta, S., Small, D. *et al.* 2019. "Association of Primary Care Clinic Appointment Time with Clinician Ordering and Patient Completion of Breast and Colorectal Cancer Screening," *JAMA Network Open* 2(5): 1–9.

Kahan, D., Peters, E., Dawson, E., & Slovic, P. 2017. "Motivated Numeracy and Enlightened Self-Government," *Behavioural Public Policy* 1(1): 54–86.

Kahneman, D. 2011. *Thinking Fast and Slow*. Farrar, Straus and Giroux.

Kahneman, D., Sibony, O., & Sunstein, C. 2021. *Noise*. Little, Brown Spark.

Kelly, T. 2005. "The Epistemic Significance of Disagreement," *Oxford Studies in Epistemology* 1: 167–196.

Kelly, T. 2010. "Peer Disagreement and Higher-Order Evidence." In Feldman & Warfield 2010, 111–174.

Kelly, T. 2013. "Disagreement and the Burdens of Judgment." In Christensen & Lackey 2013, 31–53.

Kelly, T. 2014. "Can Evidence Be Permissive?" In M. Steup, J. Turri, & E. Sosa (eds.), *Contemporary Debates in Epistemology*, 298–312. Wiley-Blackwell.

Kelly, T. 2022. *Bias*. Oxford University Press.

King, N. 2012. "Disagreement: What's the Problem? Or a Good Peer Is Hard to Find," *Philosophy and Phenomenological Research* 85(2): 249–272.

King, N. 2013. "Disagreement: The Skeptical Arguments from Peerhood and Symmetry." In Machuca 2013, 193–217.

Klein, P. 2011. "Epistemic Justification and the Limits of Pyrrhonism." In D. Machuca (ed.), *Pyrrhonism in Ancient, Modern, and Contemporary Philosophy*, 79–96. Springer.

Kornblith, H. 2010. "Belief in the Face of Controversy." In Feldman & Warfield 2010, 29–52.

Kornblith, H. 2013. "Is Philosophical Knowledge Possible?" In Machuca 2013, 260–276.

Kruger, J. & Dunning, D. 1999. "Unskilled and Unaware of It: How Difficulties in Recognizing One's Own Incompetence Lead to Inflated Self-Assessments," *Journal of Personality and Social Psychology* 77(6): 1121–1134.

Kuhn, T. 1977. "Objectivity, Value Judgment, and Theory Choice." In T. Kuhn (ed.), *The Essential Tension*, 320–339. University of Chicago Press.

Kuhn, T. 1996. *The Structure of Scientific Revolutions*. 3rd edition. University of Chicago Press.

Kukucka, J., Kassin, S., Zapf, P., & Dror, I. 2017. "Cognitive Bias and Blindness: A Global Survey of Forensic Science Examiners," *Journal of Applied Research in Memory and Cognition* 6(4): 452–459.

Kunda, Z. 1990. "The Case for Motivated Reasoning," *Psychological Bulletin* 108(3): 480–498.

Kvanvig, J. 1983. "The Evidentialist Objection," *American Philosophical Quarterly* 20(1): 47–55.

Kvanvig, J. 2021. "How to Be an Inclusivist." In M. Benton & J. Kvanvig (eds.), *Religious Disagreement and Pluralism*, 217–237. Oxford University Press.

Lackey, J. 2010. "A Justificationist View of Disagreement's Epistemic Significance." In A. Haddock, A. Millar, & D. Pritchard (eds.), *Social Epistemology*, 298–325. Oxford University Press.

Lackey, J. 2013. "Disagreement and Belief Dependence." In Christensen & Lackey 2013, 243–268.

Linder, J., Doctor, J., Friedberg, M. *et al.* (2014). "Time of Day and the Decision to Prescribe Antibiotics," *JAMA Internal Medicine* 174(12): 2029–2031.

Loftus, E. 1979. *Eyewitness Memory.* Harvard University Press.

Lord, C., Ross, L., & Lepper, M. 1979. "Biased Assimilation and Attitude Polarization: The Effects of Prior Theories on Subsequently Considered Evidence," *Journal of Personality and Social Psychology* 37(11): 2098–2109.

Lord, C. & Taylor, C. 2009. "Biased Assimilation: Effects of Assumptions and Expectations on the Interpretation of New Evidence," *Social and Personality Psychology Compass* 3(5): 827–841.

Lord, E. 2014. "From Independence to Conciliationism: An Obituary," *Australasian Journal of Philosophy* 92(2): 365–377.

Machuca, D. 2006. "The Pyrrhonist's ἀταραξία and φιλανθρωπία," *Ancient Philosophy* 26(1): 111–139.

Machuca, D. (ed.). 2013. *Disagreement and Skepticism.* Routledge.

Machuca, D. 2020. "Sextus on *Ataraxia* Revisited," *Ancient Philosophy* 40(2): 435–452.

Machuca, D. 2022. *Pyrrhonism Past and Present.* Springer.

Mackie, J. L. 1977. *Ethics.* Penguin.

Mahoney, M. 1977. "Publication Prejudices: An Experimental Study of Confirmatory Bias in the Peer Review System," *Cognitive Therapy and Research* 1(2): 161–175.

Matheson, J. 2011. "The Case for Rational Uniqueness," *Logos & Episteme* 2(3): 359–373.

Matheson, J. 2015. *The Epistemic Significance of Disagreement.* Palgrave Macmillan.

McGrath, S. 2008. "Moral Disagreement and Moral Expertise," *Oxford Studies in Metaethics* 3: 87–107.

McKim, R. 2012. *On Religious Diversity.* Oxford University Press.

Mercier, H. 2017. "Confirmation Bias – Myside Bias." In R. Pohl (ed.), *Cognitive Illusions*, 99–114. Routledge.

Moon, A. 2018. "Disagreement and New Ways to Remain Steadfast in the Face of Disagreement," *Episteme* 15(1): 65–79.

Munro, G. & Ditto, P. 1997. "Biased Assimilation, Attitude Polarization, and Affect in Reactions to Stereotype-Relevant Scientific Information," *Personality and Social Psychology Bulletin* 23(6): 636–653.

Neal, T. & Brodsky, S. 2016. "Forensic Psychologists' Perceptions of Bias and Potential Correction Strategies in Forensic Mental Health Evaluations," *Psychology, Public Policy, and Law* 22(1): 58–76.

Neprash, H. & Barnett, M. 2019. "Association of Primary Care Clinic Appointment Time with Opioid Prescribing," *JAMA Network Open* 2(8): e1910373.

Nickerson, R. 1998. "Confirmation Bias: A Ubiquitous Phenomenon in Many Guises," *Review of General Psychology* 2(2): 175–220.

Nisbett, R. & Wilson, T. 1977. "Telling More than We Can Know: Verbal Reports on Mental Processes," *Psychological Review* 84(3): 231–259.

Olivola, C. & Todorov, A. 2010. "Elected in 100 Milliseconds: Appearance-Based Trait Inferences and Voting," *Journal of Nonverbal Behavior* 34(2): 83–110.

Pasnau, R. 2015. "Disagreement and the Value of Self-Trust," *Philosophical Studies* 172(9): 2315–2339.

Philpot, L., Khokhar, B., Roellinger, D., Ramar, P., & Ebbert, J. 2018. "Time of Day Is Associated with Opioid Prescribing for Low Back Pain in Primary Care," *Journal of General Internal Medicine* 33(11): 1828–1830.

Pittard, J. 2019. *Disagreement, Deference, and Religious Commitment.* Oxford University Press.

Plantinga, A. 1993. *Warrant and Proper Function.* Oxford University Press.

Plantinga, A. 1995. "Pluralism: A Defense of Religious Exclusivism." In T. Senor (ed.), *The Rationality of Belief and the Plurality of Faith*, 191–215. Cornell University Press.

Plantinga, A. 2000. *Warranted Christian Belief.* Oxford University Press.

Pronin, E. 2007. "Perception and Misperception of Bias in Human Judgment," *Trends in Cognitive Sciences* 11(1): 37–43.

Pronin, E. 2009. "The Introspection Illusion," *Advances in Experimental Social Psychology* 41: 1–67.

Pronin, E., Gilovich, T., & Ross, L. 2004. "Objectivity in the Eye of the Beholder: Divergent Perceptions of Bias in Self versus Others," *Psychological Review* 111(3): 781–799.

Pronin, E., Kruger, J., Savitsky, K., & Ross, L. 2001. "You Don't Know Me, but I Know You: The Illusion of Asymmetric Insight," *Journal of Personality and Social Psychology* 81(4): 639–656.

Pronin, E. & Kugler, M. 2007. "Valuing Thoughts, Ignoring Behavior: The Introspection Illusion as a Source of the Bias Blind Spot," *Journal of Experimental Social Psychology* 43(4): 565–578.

Pronin, E., Lin, D., & Ross, L. 2002. "The Bias Blind Spot: Perceptions of Bias in Self and versus Others," *Personality and Social Psychology Bulletin* 28(3): 369–381.

Ranalli, C. & Thirza, L. 2022a. "Deep Disagreement (Part 1): Theories of Deep Disagreement," *Philosophy Compass* 17(12): e12886.

Ranalli, C. & Thirza, L. 2022b. "Deep Disagreement (Part 2): Epistemology of Deep Disagreement," *Philosophy Compass* 17(12): e12887.

Robinson, P., Wilson, D., Coral, A., Murphy, A., & Verow, P. 1999. "Variation between Experienced Observers in the Interpretation of Accident and Emergency Radiographs," *British Journal of Radiology* 72(856): 323–330.

Ross, L., Ehrlinger, J., & Gilovich, T. 2016. "The Bias Blind Spot and Its Implications." In K. Elsbach, A. Kayes, & D. Kayes (eds.), *Contemporary Organizational Behavior*, 137–145. Pearson.

Ross, L. & Ward, A. 1996. "Naive Realism in Everyday Life: Implications for Social Conflict and Misunderstanding." In E. Reed, E. Turiel, & T. Brown (eds.), *The Jean Piaget Symposium Series*, 103–135. Lawrence Erlbaum Associates.

Schafer, K. 2015. "How Common Is Peer Disagreement? On Self-Trust and Rational Symmetry," *Philosophy and Phenomenological Research* 91(1): 25–46.

Schnall, S., Haidt, J., Clore, G., & Jordan, A. 2008. "Disgust as Embodied Moral Judgment," *Personality and Social Psychology Bulletin* 34(8): 1096–1109.

Schnider, A. 2018. *The Confabulating Mind*. Oxford University Press.

Schoenfield, M. 2014. "Permission to Believe: Why Permissivism Is True and What It Tells Us about Irrelevant Influences on Belief," *Noûs* 48(2): 193–218.

Schoenfield, M. 2019. "Permissivism and the Value of Rationality: A Challenge to the Uniqueness Thesis," *Philosophy and Phenomenological Research* 99(2): 286–297.

Schulz, E., Cokely, E., & Feltz, A. 2011. "Persistent Bias in Expert Judgments about Free Will and Moral Responsibility: A Test of the Expertise Defense," *Consciousness and Cognition* 20(4): 1722–1731.

Schwitzgebel, E. 2011. *Perplexities of Consciousness*. The MIT Press.

Schwitzgebel, E. & Cushman, F. 2012. "Expertise in Moral Reasoning? Order Effects on Moral Judgments in Professional Philosophers and Non-philosophers," *Mind & Language* 27(2): 135–153.

Schwitzgebel, E. & Cushman, F. 2015. "Philosophers' Biased Judgments Persist despite Training, Expertise and Reflection," *Cognition* 141: 127–137.

Scopelliti, I., Morewedge, C., McCormick, E. *et al.* 2015. "Bias Blind Spot: Structure, Measurement, and Consequences," *Management Science* 61(10): 2468–2486.

Sherman, B. 2015. "Questionable Peers and Spinelessness," *Canadian Journal of Philosophy* 45(4): 425–444.

Sidgwick, H. 1874. *The Methods of Ethics*. Macmillan.

Sidgwick, H. 1895. "The Philosophy of Common Sense," *Mind* 4(14): 145–158.

Sidgwick, H. 1905. Apendix to "Criteria of Truth and Error." In H. Sidgwick (ed.), *Lectures on the Philosophy of Kant and Other Philosophical Lectures and Essays*, 461–467. Macmillan.

Sosa, E. 2010. "The Epistemology of Disagreement." In A. Haddock, A. Millar, & D. Pritchard (eds.), *Social Epistemology*, 278–297. Oxford University Press.

Stanovich, K. 2021. *The Bias that Divides Us*. The MIT Press.

Tobia, K., Buckwalter, W., & Stich, S. 2013. "Moral Intuitions: Are Philosophers Experts?" *Philosophical Psychology* 26(5): 629–638.

Tobia, K., Chapman, G., & Stich, S. 2013. "Cleanliness Is Next to Morality, Even for Philosophers," *Journal of Consciousness Studies* 20(11–12): 195–204.

Todorov, A., Mandisodza, A., Goren, A., & Hall, C. 2005. "Inferences of Competence from Faces Predict Election Outcomes," *Science* 308(5728): 1623–1626.

Ulery, B., Hicklin, R., Buscaglia, J., & Roberts, M. 2012. "Repeatability and Reproducibility of Decisions by Latent Fingerprint Examiners," *PLoS One* 7(2): e32800.

Vaesen, K., Peterson, M., & van Bezooijen, B. 2013. "The Reliability of Armchair Intuitions," *Metaphilosophy* 44(5): 559–578.

van Inwagen, P. 1996. "It Is Wrong, Everywhere, Always, and for Anyone, to Believe Anything upon Insufficient Evidence." In J. Jordan & D. Howard-Snyder (eds.), *Faith, Freedom, and Rationality*, 137–153. Rowman & Littlefield.

van Inwagen, P. 2010. "We're Right. They're Wrong." In Feldman & Warfield 2010, 10–28.

Walker, M. 2023. *Outlines of Skeptical-Dogmatism*. Lexington Books.

Weatherson, B. 2013. "Disagreements, Philosophical and Otherwise." In Christensen & Lackey 2013, 54–73.

Weatherson, B. 2019. *Normative Externalism*. Oxford University Press.

Wedgwood, R. 2007. *The Nature of Normativity*. Oxford University Press.

Wedgwood, R. 2010. "The Moral Evil Demons." In Feldman & Warfield 2010, 216–246.

West, K. & Eaton, A. 2019. "Prejudiced and Unaware of It: Evidence for the Dunning-Kruger Model in the Domains of Racism and Sexism," *Personality and Individual Differences* 146: 111–119.

West, R., Meserve, R., & Stanovich, K. 2012. "Cognitive Sophistication Does Not Attenuate the Bias Blind Spot," *Journal of Personality and Social Psychology* 103(3): 506–519.

Wheatley, T. 2009. "Everyday Confabulation." In W. Hirstein (ed.), *Confabulation*, 203–221. Oxford University Press.

Wheatley, T. & Haidt, J. 2005. "Hypnotically Induced Disgust Makes Moral Judgments More Severe," *Psychological Science* 16(10): 780–784.

White, R. 2005. "Epistemic Permissiveness," *Philosophical Perspectives* 19: 445–459.

White, R. 2014. "Evidence Cannot Be Permissive." In M. Steup, J. Turri, & E. Sosa (eds.), *Contemporary Debates in Epistemology*, 312–323. Wiley-Blackwell.

Williams, M. 2004. "The Agrippan Argument and Two Forms of Skepticism." In W. Sinnott-Armstrong (ed.), *Pyrrhonian Skepticism*, 121–145. Oxford University Press.

Wilson, T. 2002. *Strangers to Ourselves*. Harvard University Press.

Wilson, T. & Brekke, N. 1994. "Mental Contamination and Mental Correction: Unwanted Influences on Judgments and Evaluations," *Psychological Bulletin* 116(1): 117–142.

Wilson, T. & Nisbett, R. 1978. "The Accuracy of Verbal Reports about the Effects of Stimuli on Evaluations and Behavior," *Social Psychology* 41(2): 118–131.

Wittgenstein, L. 1969. *On Certainty*. Blackwell.

Acknowledgments

I would like to thank Stephen Hetherington for the invitation to author this Element. Two anonymous reviewers provided very helpful comments, for which I am grateful. Work on the Element was possible thanks in part to a Senior Fellowship at the Maimonides Centre for Advanced Studies (DFG-FOR 2311), Hamburg University.

Cambridge Elements ⹀

Epistemology

Stephen Hetherington
University of New South Wales, Sydney

Stephen Hetherington is Professor Emeritus of Philosophy at the University of New South Wales, Sydney. He is the author of numerous books, including *Knowledge and the Gettier Problem* (Cambridge University Press, 2016) and *What Is Epistemology?* (Polity, 2019), and is the editor of several others, including *Knowledge in Contemporary Epistemology* (with Markos Valaris: Bloomsbury, 2019) and *What the Ancients Offer to Contemporary Epistemology* (with Nicholas D. Smith: Routledge, 2020). He was the Editor-in-Chief of the Australasian Journal of Philosophy from 2013 until 2022.

About the Series
This Elements series seeks to cover all aspects of a rapidly evolving field, including emerging and evolving topics such as: fallibilism; knowinghow; self-knowledge; knowledge of morality; knowledge and injustice; formal epistemology; knowledge and religion; scientific knowledge; collective epistemology; applied epistemology; virtue epistemology; wisdom. The series demonstrates the liveliness and diversity of the field, while also pointing to new areas of investigation.

Cambridge Elements ☰

Epistemology

Elements in the Series

A full series listing is available at: www.cambridge.org/EEPI

Printed in the United States
by Baker & Taylor Publisher Services